Grace & Speed

Grace & Speed

PAINTINGS BY **DOUG DUNFORD**

TEXT BY **ANDREW WAGNER-CHAZALON**

Algonquin International

© 2006 Andrew Wagner-Chazalon and Doug Dunford

Published in 2006 by
Algonquin International Limited
505 Highway 118 West — Suite 160
Bracebridge, Ontario P1L 2G7

Distributed by
Muskoka Wooden Boat Memories
A Division of Muskoka Print & Poster Company
Box 571, Gravenhurst, Ontario   P1P 1E4
www.woodenboatmemories.com

Library and Archives Canada Cataloguing in Publication

Dunford, Doug, 1953–
Grace & speed / paintings by Doug Dunford ;
text by Andrew Wagner-Chazalon.

Includes bibliographical references and index.
ISBN 0-9780362-0-4

1. Wooden boats — Ontario — Muskoka (District municipality) — History.
2. Boats and boating — Ontario — District municipality — History.
I. Wagner-Chazalon, Andrew, 1966– II. Title.   III. Title: Grace and speed.

VM341.D854 2006   623.82'07   C2006-901251-2

Design by Gillian Stead
Editing by Lynn Roberts
Photography by Kelly Holinshead / The Shutterbug Gallery, Huntsville

Printed in Singapore

Contents

For Murray, a genuine friend who truly believed in me;
For Jill, who has been an enormous support;
For Dylan, Jordan and Simon, who brighten my world.

D. A. D.

❖ ❖ ❖

For Betty Chazalon and David Chazalon.
Through your books and your stories you taught me
that boats are important, and that life on the water matters.

A. W.-C.

Foreword

Back in the 1970s when I was an art teacher in Burlington, a young man from a neighbouring school dropped by after classes. His name was Doug Dunford, whose reputation preceded him. A glance at his portfolio convinced me of his outstanding talent. Through the years he has honed his skills and found his niche. Any artist worth his salt paints what is in his heart. Doug's work is an outstanding testimonial to his love for the picturesque Muskoka landscape and its heritage.

From the early 20th century educated people of taste made Muskoka their summer home. They were able to afford the finest craftmanship in their pioneering powerboats. What a perfect combination of the land of lakes and the superb craft to explore those lakes. It was a combination felt deeply in the hearts of those who experienced it. Now Doug Dunford has touched that spiritual core with his fresh and vivid art.

Robert Bateman

1

A Place Like No Other

"No speedboat builders in the world ever surpassed the Canadians"

When you summer in Muskoka, it can be easy to take the beauty of its wooden boats for granted. Spend a sunny Saturday afternoon on the lakes and you are likely to see a gorgeous old launch cruising sedately past, or catch a glimpse of a gleaming gentleman's racer skipping across the surface, the spray glistening on its varnished mahogany. Familiarity, in this case, does not breed contempt — the grand old boats are much too beautiful to ever be viewed that way — but it is easy to take them for granted, to forget just how rich and rare this resource is. But the truth is that there are few other places that can rival this relatively small district for its abundance of wooden boats, and none that can surpass the quality of those boats. Certainly there is nowhere else in Canada that

even comes close, and most of the boating centres in the U.S. — Lake Tahoe, Lake Geneva, and a handful of others — have more than a few Muskoka-built boats adding to the beauty of their waterways.

Muskoka is the place where the art of building wooden boats reached a pinnacle of artistry not exceeded anywhere else. Joseph Gribbins, a leader among American boating writers, put it this way: "No speedboat builders in the world ever surpassed the Canadians, whose boats are perfect in line, detail, craftsmanship, finish and pure style." And to an American fan of wooden boats, "Canadians" means "Muskokans." For a few decades, most of the top boat builders and designers in the country gathered in this region and produced some of their finest work. There are other regions where

boats have been produced, of course, boats of great beauty and renown. But no other area, and certainly no other area of similar size and population, has produced as many boats of such surpassing quality as Muskoka.

Muskoka was destined by geography to be a region of boat-lovers. There's almost as much water in the region as there is land, with a dozen rivers and hundreds of lakes making travel by boat easy and convenient. That was particularly true in the early years of settlement here, when the rocky nature of the land made roads difficult to build, expensive to maintain, and unpleasant to travel. In those years, boats were not just a pleasant diversion, they were an essential means of transportation.

There are plenty of other regions with an abundance of waterways, but Muskoka had three elements that conspired to take boat building here to heights not seen elsewhere: a skilled workforce, visionary leaders, and a committed clientele.

The workforce developed here in part because Muskoka was settled in an unusual way. Most other areas that are now known as "cottage country" grew according to a familiar pattern: first came the loggers in their temporary camps; then the settlers began carving out farms and establishing villages; and then came the cottagers, fleeing the oppressive atmosphere of late 19th century cities and seeking fresh air for their summer holidays. All those groups were also found in Muskoka, but their arrival pattern was compressed. The region wasn't opened up to settlement until the late 1850s, and vacationers, loggers, entrepreneurs and would-be farmers began pouring in here at the same time. For a few years there was a tremendous amount of juggling as the permanent residents tried to figure out how to make a living. Farming was a viable option only for those few who had good land on their parcel of property, but hotels soon started springing up and many lakeside farmhouses became guest houses and then resorts. Some hotel guests decided they'd like to have a place of their own, and a boat to use while they were there, and any man who could swing a hammer and cut a straight line soon learned that he could make a much better living building cottages in the summer and boats in the winter than he could ever hope to make by farming the unyielding rock.

By the time boat building moved beyond the backyard shop and into professional boatyards, Muskoka had an abundance of skilled men who had already spent years building boats. They knew how to steam and bend ribs and how to scour a lumber pile for the right piece of wood for carving a stem. Just as importantly, they had found in themselves a passion for boat building. They knew the satisfaction that came from producing a vessel with clean lines that satisfied the eye when it was on land, and which handled well on the water. They would rather build boats than anything else, and they were prepared to do whatever it took to keep building boats.

Then there were the geniuses, the men of extraordinary talent or vision who were able to guide boat building in a new direction. Throughout history there have been regions where one art form or another thrived — painting in 17th century Holland, poetry in the lake country of Wordsworth and Keats, theatre in Shakespearean London. It's debatable whether these times produced the geniuses, or whether the influence works the other way around, but it is certain that a towering presence like Shakespeare has a profound influence on his peers. The artistic genius doesn't just create surpassing works, he inspires his contemporaries by showing new ways of doing things, and by setting a high standard and challenging those around him to surpass it. The effect is compounded when there are several artists creating work of exceptional beauty, as they begin to compete with each other and drive the standards of their craft even higher. That certainly happened in Muskoka. The region would still have been a boat building centre without Bert Minett, Herb Ditchburn, or Tom Greavette, but it would almost certainly have been a lesser centre, producing boats that did not meet the standard we know today.

But even with the workers and the visionaries, Muskoka would not have reached the heights it did were it not for the clients. A writer can labour for years in his solitary garret, producing works of great genius for no more than the cost of a pen and some paper, but boat builders work in a different medium, and a great vessel can only be produced with great wood and superior fittings. If the boat is motorized, the engine must also be of surpassing quality, which usually means it must be the latest model. None of these components come cheaply. Fine wood is expensive, and selecting it requires a willingness to reject anything that isn't quite good enough. Turning that wood into something beautiful is a process that can't be rushed, for even the most skilled workman must be given the time to achieve a high level of craft. Fittings must be custom made, the molds carved from soft pine then sent to a foundry to be cast, ground, plated and polished. Varnish must be applied again and again and again if the boat is to gleam as it should. Even at 75 cents an hour — the going rate for a boat builder in 1932 — building a boat is an expensive proposition; building a great one is even more costly.

Muskoka had more than its share of wealthy residents, multi-millionaires from the steel mills and banks of Pittsburgh and Toronto, and Canadian royalty like the Eatons. They understood art forms and design — in their urban homes they were surrounded by fine art and architecture, and many of them were patrons of various arts. They lost none of their taste when they came to the cottage: Muskoka's deep-pocketed people were willing to spend their money on boats. They were cognoscente who recognized the value of selecting mahogany so the deck boards all have the same grain, or installing an engraved silver dash plate rather than a simple wooden one. They saw each other at social functions and while cruising the lakes, and they were keenly aware of each other's boats. Many of them did not just want to have a fine boat, they wanted to have the finest, the fastest, the most luxurious boat on the lakes, and they were willing to pay to get it.

The result was a fiercely competitive atmosphere, in which boat shops filled with extraordinarily talented people laboured constantly to outdo each other. A single letter from Herb Ditchburn underlines the spirit in which boats were being built. On July 2, 1929, he responded to a complaint from one of his customers, Fred Burgess, who had purchased a new Viking model earlier that year. Burgess had called Ditchburn on Dominion Day after seeing another Viking which belonged to Lady Eaton, and deciding that his new boat wasn't built to as high a standard as hers. Ditchburn invited Burgess to bring in the boat that week for minor repairs and measurements, and to return it to the shop in the fall for a three-week refit. "We will at this time bring it up to the finish of the very best jobs that we have turned out to date, and possibly better," Ditchburn wrote.

Burgess may have been comparing his Ditchburn boat to another, but Herb Ditchburn knew who he was really competing with. Clients like Fred Burgess were perfectly aware that there were several other builders on the same lakes who would be only too happy to build them a new boat, and who were capable of approaching, or even exceeding, Ditchburn's standards. "We appreciate that your boat is being used alongside some of our competitors' best," Ditchburn wrote, "and are therefore anxious to bring it into a condition which will leave no room for criticism."

Visionary designers and skilled builders, wealthy customers willing to foot the bill, and a desire to build boats that would "leave no room for criticism." It was the perfect combination of elements, the potent brew that was guaranteed to make Muskoka a boat building centre like no other.

More than a century after the first boatworks opened in Muskoka, the region's residents retain an unparalleled fleet of wooden boats. Many have been treasured by the descendants of their original owners; others have been rediscovered and revived by the new cognoscente, people who understand the unique beauty of these vessels and who are willing to spend hundreds of thousands of dollars to restore a single boat to immaculate condition. The price of the boats can be measured — a number of boats have sold for more than a million dollars — but, as with any work of art, the real value is beyond price. The boats of Muskoka are a unique treasure. They are, quite simply, the finest wooden motorboats ever .

2 Capturing the Artistry

One afternoon in the early 1970s, a teacher walked into his high school art class in Burlington, placed an apple on the table, and told his students to draw it. For the next hour the students dutifully worked, silently trying to copy the apple while the teacher watched in growing frustration. At the end of the class he smashed a pointer, shattering it on the desk. "You all fail," he fumed.

Not one of his students had picked up the apple, he raged. Nobody had smelled it, tasted it. All of them had looked at it, recognized it as an apple, and drawn from their memories of what apples were like.

That single lesson had a profound impact on a young art student named Doug Dunford. More than thirty years later, he's still using the lesson taught in that Burlington high school classroom. Only now, instead of applying it to apples, he's applying it to boats and water.

It's a delicate balancing act for a painter to capture both the general and the specific of his subject. That's particularly true when he's painting something which already has a defined character — a portrait of a person, for example, or a boat. The painter has to see his subject in two different ways: it is a boat which floats and moves in a particular way, and it is a collection of angles and lines and colours. "When we walk down the street, we see 'sidewalk,' 'grass,' 'brick house.' We put words to things," Dunford explains. "I don't think 'boat.' I see colours, I see the form. Each one has a unique form, its own negative and positive tones, its values, its form." At the same time he manages to embrace the boat as an entire creation, as a vessel whose builders gave it both artistry and purpose and whose owners imbue it with character and life.

There are plenty of people who paint old boats, but there are few — if any — who paint them as well as Dunford. There is a level of sophistication in his boat paintings which move them far beyond mere illustrations of the vessels: they are artistic creations that convey meaning, tell stories, evoke an emotional response. There is authority in his paintings, an authenticity that comes from somebody who has not only mastered the technical requirements of realist painting — the "stitchery" as Dunford calls it — but who truly understands the subject he is painting. He doesn't just know what a boat looks like, he knows how it sounds first thing in the morning, what it smells like when the sun warms the varnish, how it behaves when heeled over in a hard left turn at forty miles an hour; he understands its personality.

Dunford has long been known for his paintings of Muskoka, which are displayed in framed prints that seem to hang in nearly every cottage and boathouse, but his fame has begun to spread far beyond the region. His paintings continue to rise in value, and originals are being sold for far more than they were originally sold for. More importantly, his works are being coveted and regarded seriously as the work of a painter with something to say.

Dunford may be renowned as a painter of boats, but the water is often the first thing you notice in his paintings, a background so compelling that the eye drinks it in for a while before moving to the boat which is the ostensible subject of the painting. The water — and in particular the freshwater of central Ontario — is Dunford's natural environment, and he captures it with the accuracy of one who has known and loved it in all seasons.

Dunford grew up spending summers beside the water. His grandparents had a property on Clear Lake in Haliburton, a typical all-purpose spot of the type that still thrived in the 1950s, combining a marina, a boat repair shop, a coffee shop and about a hundred campsites. "That was how I spent all my summers, water-skiing, fishing, shooting frogs, harassing the bears in the dump, meeting girls," said Dunford. "All my experiences as a child were around the water, around the cottage."

The other ten months of the year were spent in Burlington, attending school and gradually coming to the realization that he was an artist. One of his early teachers there was Robert Bateman, who taught classes at Lord Elgin High School. On weekends, Dunford and a group of other young art students would gather at Bateman's home near the Bruce Trail for hikes and nature walks, followed by discussions and painting sessions in his studio. Dunford learned technique from Bateman, but he also learned to look deeper into his subject, to see whatever he was painting as an element in a larger environment rather than to create an artificial divide between background and subject. That, too, was a lesson he would continue to apply.

Like many young artists, Dunford travelled widely after school. He spent time on British Columbia's Saltspring Island and in Bali, and lived for a while in Algonquin Park. He sold whatever paintings he could, and took other jobs to make money. For a few years he worked at a commercial gallery and framing shop in Hamilton, framing art, making deliveries, sweeping the floor. One day he brought in some of his own work to frame, watercolours of the local countryside. The gallery owner recognized its commercial value and told Dunford to stop making deliveries and start painting. "I'll buy everything you can produce," he said, and the young artist responded with enthusiasm. "I was doing watercolours for fifty bucks a pop. I'd whip outside of Hamilton, find a farm scene, go click-click with the camera, go back to town and paint."

It was exhilarating and lucrative at first, but Dunford soon found the work to be tiresome, and began looking for something that reflected his own personality.

"After I quit painting barn scenes I went through a period where it was all people," Dunford said. "A linesman going up a pole, with his tools in his belt. It was all detail, detail. I was going to wow people, to show them a painting that was so real."

He knew he was getting closer to what he really wanted to paint, but he hadn't yet found it. He hadn't yet realized that his true subject matter, his "authentic self," wasn't to be found on land.

⬧ ⬧ ⬧

There is a solitude on the lake in the early morning, or at least the illusion of solitude. It's quiet once the sun peeks above the horizon and the birds cease their vigorous pre-dawn chorus, and for a brief time, everyone whose eyes are open at dawn feels that the lake belongs to them and them alone. It doesn't, of course, for the water in Muskoka is always a shared experience. The wakeboarders and the water-skiers may still be asleep, but the lake belongs to all those who are compelled to rise early: the building contractors and the die-hard anglers, the early-rising elderly and the insomniacs.

And the artists.

Early morning has always been a time for artists, who seek the dramatic light and colours that disappear as the sun rises higher. There is pink there, definitely a dusty, rosey pink, but there's much more than that. Greens and purples mingle, and blues dance along the shoreline. The colours refuse to stay still, though, shifting and jumping hues and tones and values as the sun rises higher.

Doug Dunford has painted the lake at this hour many times. In fact he rarely sees it in the afternoon now, choosing to go on the water only in the early morning or the late afternoon and evening. "It's too harsh in the afternoon," he says. "Everything turns to spaghetti."

This morning he's on the lake with his friend Murray Walker, a lover of art and of wooden boats. They're in one of Walker's boats, a gorgeous Minett-Shields launch, and the sun is just up when they begin their cruise of Lake Rosseau. Dunford is particularly keen to see some islands this morning, ones that have the sun behind them so he can study once again how the light and shadow play on the water. Walker pilots the boat, studying the chart for water depth as they enter a few bays he's unfamiliar with, while Dunford looks and

photographs. He captures a few images around Harraby Point where the sun silhouettes an island and makes the rippling water glisten with gold, but he hasn't yet found what he's looking for.

It is a hot morning, the air already pregnant with the promise of an afternoon thunderstorm. Away to the east, where the sun has climbed above the horizon, the haze colours the land various shades of the same grey-green. The near islands are dark, the distant points are lighter, the far hills so pale they nearly blend in with the dust-filled sky. Dunford stares at the scene for a few moments, then takes a picture for future reference. "I love those different values," he says quietly.

The cruise is nearly over when they find it, the dramatic shot they'd been hoping for. On the north side of an island is an old wooden boathouse. Through one door can be seen three cypress rowing skiffs, their hulls gleaming in the rising sunlight.

"Look at that!" Dunford says, and begins shooting the scene. Walker cruises past, then circles to cruise past again.

A minute later, passing to the south of the island, Dunford sees another image that cries out to him, a pine-decked point silhouetted by the sun. Again he shoots. "I'll probably take the boathouse out of that, but I'll use that pine point," he says.

This is Dunford's subject matter, and he vividly recalls the day he first found it. It was 1974, and he was house-sitting for a friend in Muskoka when somebody offered to take him for a boat cruise. "It was one of those calm mornings when everything is reflected in the water," he said, "and Bang! There I am. My authentic self."

"After that, every time I went out on the lake I'd see a million paintings. People playing on the beach, a boathouse. A water-skier would go by and I'd say 'whoa!' Look at the plume of water!"

He began painting the water obsessively, and soon found he had produced two hundred paintings — enough to have a solo show at a

Muskoka gallery. He wondered if any of the pieces would sell. All of them did.

He took notice of the Muskoka chairs that perched on every other dock, admired their lines and the way they caught the light. The chairs were manmade, but they seemed to have become as much a part of the environment as the trees and water and rocks. He painted a pair of them, called the painting Old Friends, and had a print made from it. It has gone through seven reprintings, and become one of the best-known images of Muskoka. He painted more chairs, more boats, more boathouses. And with each painting, and with each morning spent on the lake, he became a better painter of water.

If you begin painting water by thinking about the waves, he says, you are going to end up with something artificial and static, something that is most unlike water. Even on the most calm day, there is movement in the water, a rise and fall that gives it an ever-changing structure. "I look at water as more like a landscape. There are hills and valleys, and each one is different. Water has structure, not only the individual waves but the whole surface. It's not just a bunch of brush strokes going from one end to the other."

"You've got to feel the water, to understand that one part of it is going up while another is going down. You've got to understand its movement."

And, just as the young art students did when painting an apple, you have to stop thinking of it as water. "When I paint water, it's like writing a letter. Each wave is a word, and you can't just write the same word over and over again."

A passionate musician, Dunford reaches to music for another analogy. "I studied music for years, played it for years. Then one day I had a breakthrough. I realized I wasn't even thinking about whether I needed to play a C or a B chord next. You become the music — it's all just something that happens to you."

There are a lot of things that can get in the way of that process, though, a lot of thoughts that can intrude. To paint water well, you need the same degree of technical skill as a musician who no longer needs to think about which chord comes next in the progression. You also need to have spent hours meditating on water, watching its movements and feeling its moods, so well that you can feel its structure even when the wind is pelting snow against the windows of the studio, and the only lake in sight is the one you captured in a photograph. Only then can you stop thinking long enough to do.

"To do a good painting, you have to live in the now with that painting. When I'm painting waves, it's nothingness. If I think about it, it gets calculated, the words get in the way."

❖ ❖ ❖

It's a cold November afternoon, the lakes are slowly freezing over, and Dunford is working in the studio behind his home north of Bracebridge. The water on this painting — an image of Ted Rogers's late model Greavette — is complete and Dunford is working on the boat itself. Again and again he goes over the hull, subtly adjusting the shade and lines until he's satisfied that the painting reflects both the look and the feel of the boat.

Part of the challenge in painting boats, he says, is to make them accurate and artistic at the same time. "Right from the beginning of doing these boats, I wanted to try with all my power not to make them illustrations but to make them paintings," he said.

"I try to go after its history, its spiritual content, its visual content in a different way than a photographer would. It's about how the boat fits into its world." It's another lesson he learned in his youth, this one from Robert Bateman: in order to capture the spirit of the subject, you need to show it in its natural environment.

It helps that the subjects he's painting are so perfectly matched to that environment. Even though he strives to think of his subjects as structures of form and line, colour and shade, Dunford also can't help but admire the beauty of the boats as boats. "The boat builders who did well, they understood the wood and the water. They were at one with the boat, the form of the boat and how it would go through the water."

There is a beauty to them — not merely craftsmanship, but an artistic beauty — and painting a well-made boat, Dunford says, is very much like painting a work of nature. "When I paint nature, I'm just duplicating the real art. Mother Nature is the artist. I try to capture it and put my feelings into it, but I can't go wrong because nature's such a beautiful thing."

"The better you can be in tune and balance with that visual content, the closer you're going to get to the real thing. It's the same with the boats."

A large boat like Rita is meant to carry a crowd. On the day Dunford arrived to photograph the boat, the owners were preparing to take guests aboard for a picnic excursion. The moment was perfect, and Rita was painted doing what she does best. The white hull, portholes and mast give this boat an almost Caribbean look, but the low freeboard reveals that it was built for the more protected waters of Muskoka.

3

Bert Minett: A Craftsman's Craftsman

Nobody knows for sure how many boat builders were working in Muskoka in the years before First World War. Likely dozens, if one includes all the people who spent their summers farming or running resorts or renting rowboats, and their winters building a boat or two which they could sell to tourists the next year. But in all that crowded field, there were two firms that stood above the rest, two builders who could be counted on to produce the very finest boats of any kind: in Gravenhurst there was Ditchburn, and in Bracebridge there was Minett.

Hubert Charles Minett was born in 1881 on his family's Lake Rosseau farm, the farm which would become Clevelands House Resort. Raised on the water, it is not surprising that he soon showed a fascination with boats. While he was still a teenager he began building boats in the barn, and by the time he was 22 his accomplishments included a 45-foot steam launch and a number of boats equipped with primitive gas engines. Recognizing that he needed some more training if he was to progress in his chosen field, Minett left Muskoka for a time and travelled to Michigan to work for the best boat designer of his generation, John L. Hacker.

Only four years Minett's senior, Hacker was already recognized as a superb boat architect. Like Minett, Hacker had begun building boats as a teenager. But while his young protégé grew up in the backwoods of Muskoka, Hacker was raised in Detroit, a hub of mechanical genius. Working as a bookkeeper in his father's business by day,

Hacker took naval architecture courses at night school. He spent his off hours visiting boatyards and machine shops, getting to know some of the other mechanical tinkerers in the area, people like Henry Ford, the Dodge brothers, and Christopher Columbus Smith who was experimenting with Naphtha engines and would later go on to found the world's largest boat building firm, Chris-Craft. In 1903, when Bert Minett was teaching himself how to build a steamboat on the beach at Clevelands House, John Hacker was designing and building a 32-and-a-half-foot boat that could travel 23 miles an hour, making it the fastest boat of its size in the U.S.

Minett spent two years working for Hacker, studied sailboat design briefly in Boston, then returned to Muskoka. In late 1910, he set up shop just above the falls in Bracebridge and H.C. Minett Motorboat Works was born. Minett was soon attracting orders from knowledgeable boat owners who recognized his skills and valued fine work. Among them was William L. Mellon of Squirrel Island on Lake Muskoka. Already wealthy thanks to a family history of banking and industry, Mellon's wealth had grown dramatically when he helped found Gulf Oil. In 1909 he came to visit his cousin in Muskoka, and the next year he and a friend purchased Squirrel Island. Around the same time he commissioned Minett to build a pair of motor launches, likely for use by his staff.

The two boats, *Skipjack* and *Floss*, are small and elegant craft. Eighteen feet long, with a dainty canoe stern and a straight stem at the bow, they were built with oak frames and ribs covered with cypress planks on *Floss* and cedar planks on *Skipjack*. The woodwork on both boats is impeccable, with touches that show Minett's attention to detail and his ability to take pride in the artistic form of his boats as well as their function. Some of the work is subtle — the oak coaming board that arcs around the boat is slightly higher at the bow and stern, creating a line that mimics the sheerline — but their overall effect is to make what would have been a lovely boat even more pleasing to the eye.

The configuration of both boats is highly reminiscent of the small steam launches that had been built a decade earlier, with leather-upholstered bench seats around the outside and the engine fitted in the middle. But steam engines were out of fashion by 1909, and it certainly would have been inappropriate for a man who'd made a fortune in oil to run his boats on anything but gasoline, so both boats were powered by gasoline engines. With no boiler taking up precious space, they could each carry six adults in comfort, or quantities of vegetables and other supplies which the staff of Squirrel Island required to keep their employers comfortable.

Forward motion on the *Floss* is controlled by two variable pitch propellers mounted on a single shaft. A second shaft inside the first adjusts the pitch of each propeller, allowing the boat to remain motionless or move in reverse without need for a transmission.

If Minett had built only this sort of boat, he would have been remembered as a skilled craftsman. But he was much more versatile than that, and in those years before the war an astonishing variety of boats flowed out of his shop.

As motors improved, both in power and reliability, people began to put a premium on speed. A fast boat was a good boat. Boats weren't being sold as stock models, so having the fastest boat on the lake was a sign that you knew what you were doing when you commissioned your boat. You had selected the right boat builder, chosen a good design, and you had the money to purchase a powerful engine and have your boat built to exacting standards. Speed became a status symbol, and Minett was always willing to help his clients increase their status.

In 1914, G.V. Foreman of Cliff Island commissioned Minett to build the fastest launch on the lake, a boat which would go faster than Minett's 1911 launch, *Norwood II*. The result was *Tango*. Thirty-two feet long with a lightweight cedar hull that was painted black, *Tango* was quickly recognized as a boat that was not only fast, but clean in the water. Like all launches of its era it is narrow and sharp-ended, but *Tango* has a slightly wider stern than some of its contemporaries. The result is a boat that sits well in the water at any speed, keeping its nose down as it accelerates, and throwing remarkably little spray or wake. If Lake Muskoka was butter, *Tango* would be a hot knife. In keeping with its performance, the lines are simple and uncluttered, the hardware minimal. Designed by Bert Hawker, who worked for Minett until he went overseas during the First World War, it achieved its goal: it was indeed the fastest boat on the lakes.

Around the same time as *Tango* was being built, Minett and his crew were working on another, very different type of boat. The hull for *Rita* was built in 1911, stamped with Minett's maker's plate and serial number 6. But something happened — if there was a deal to turn the hull into a boat, it fell through, and for two years the enormous hull occupied space in Minett's shop. Then, around 1913, Carl Borntraeger paid a visit, saw the hull and commissioned a boat. Borntraeger knew what he was doing. A lover of mechanical devices, he would later learn to fly and often hosted ace pilot Billy Bishop at his summer home on Cinderwood Island. He was already a knowledgeable boat owner with training in naval engineering, and his summer home was located less than half a mile from Squirrel Island, the

Early in the morning the water colour changes rapidly as the sun comes up. Colours such as this rich green are rarely seen by those who sleep late, but Dunford knows it well. Early morning is one of his favourite times to be on the water. On such a morning, Tango slips quickly through the lake. Its speed is deceptive, as the narrow hull and soft chine produce very little wake.

summer home of the Mellon family who had commissioned *Floss* and *Skipjack*. He had several boats on the island and over the years would add many more, including speedboats like *B-IV* which was named for the four Borntraeger children. He knew a good boat when he saw one, and he knew a good boat builder, so it was no accident that brought him to Bert Minett's shop.

Perhaps because the hull was taking up space in the shop, Minett agreed to build the boat for a bargain price — $7,500 for the 50-foot boat, compared to $2,500 he was paid for *Tango*. But Minett wasn't one to skimp on the work just because the profit wasn't there, and he built a boat that was worthy of the name Minett. The boat, to be named for Borntraeger's wife, Marguerite, would be used as a picnic boat and as a transport to bring the family and their luggage from the train station at Gravenhurst to the island. It would need to be enclosed, so they could travel to the island no matter what the weather when they arrived in Gravenhurst, and it would need to be comfortable for a family that had just travelled by train from Pittsburgh. For picnics it would require a galley and a head, and plenty of storage for food and dishes.

As usual, Minett outdid himself. The interior woodwork was nothing less than spectacular, with gleaming mahogany from one end of the below-decks cabin to the other. The cabinet work was meticulous, and 90 years later drawers open and close effortlessly, and the

AT LEFT: *One of Dunford's most popular paintings, and one that has been sold around the world in print form, this painting doesn't just capture the look of the* Floss, *it also conveys the peacefulness and tranquil mode of living such a boat evokes. A rare watercolour, this boat was painted using the dry brush technique in which very little moisture is used to apply the paint. The result is a painting with the translucence and lightness of a watercolour, yet with plenty of the rich details one expects from a Dunford painting.*

pocket doors which can be pulled out of the floor to enclose the cabin slide up and into place perfectly despite not having been used in decades. The hull and the 200 horsepower Sterling engine were well matched, and the *Rita* slides through the water with enough speed that people have water-skied behind her.

Like a surprising number of Minett's early boats, *Rita* continues to ply the waters. Unlike some of the others, she remains in the same boathouse she has always known. A rambling structure with slips and storage rooms tucked around every corner, the boathouse on Cinderwood Island bears little resemblance to the dainty designs favoured by modern architects. This is a boat-lover's boathouse, a building whose charm comes from its unity of purpose rather than from any niceties of décor. The air is rich with the scent of water and oil, wood and rope, canvas and varnish. A room on the second floor is full of engine parts, the bits and pieces that are needed to maintain the old boats, the old water pumps, and any other bits of machinery that need to be repaired. Downstairs is the boatman's office, a wood stove in one corner, scraps of paper tacked to the walls as reminders of tasks that were completed long ago. Pencil jottings on a nearby door mark the comings and goings of *Rita*, her launch dates and maintenance schedule. "Put the Rita in the water, May 8 1948," reads one entry. "Snow like hell." And looking perfectly at home amid it all, as beautiful as the day she was launched, sits *Rita*.

The people who brought this boat to life are long dead. Two generations of mechanics and refinishers who maintained this boat have come and gone. Most of the boats that were afloat when *Rita*, *Tango*, *Floss*, and *Skipjack* were launched have vanished and been forgotten. But these boats, and some of the other early boats of Bert Minett, continue to delight their owners. They remain what they always were, the superb works of a master craftsman. They remain cherished.

It's not unusual for Dunford to paint a boat like Wasan *several times in order to show different details, different lines.
Boats are complex and lovely creations, and even the best painting can only capture so many elements of them at once.
Selecting which elements to choose is one of the things that moves a painting from mere illustration into artistry.*

4   Ditchburn: A Name to Reckon With

Among the boat lovers of Muskoka, the debate often rages about which boat builder was the best. Minett, say some, citing his famed attention to detail. Greavette, others insist, pointing to innovative craft such as the instantly-recognizable Streamliner. Others champion independent builders like Clive Brown who pursued the path of solitary craftsmanship. But move beyond the closeted world of Muskoka boat fans, and there's one name that resonates above the rest. One boat owner tells of meeting people from Saskatchewan who knew only one thing about Muskoka, that there had once been a boat builder there: "Ditch-something," they said.

Ditchburn was among the first, was certainly the largest, and was in many eyes the best of the Muskoka boat builders. More than just a small boat shop, it was a firm renowned for building some of the finest pleasure craft ever launched anywhere. It had its beginnings in Rosseau in the 1870s, where four brothers had been living the life typical of many early settlers in Muskoka: middle-class immigrants from Britain, they'd arrived with big hopes and few agricultural skills, then struggled to make a living by farming poor land and working at whatever jobs they could find or create. When a grand hotel known as Rosseau House opened in the middle of their remote and rustic village, the Ditchburn brothers found their calling. One became the hotel clerk, and the others began building rowboats to rent to hotel guests.

They soon had boat liveries on Lake Joseph, at Port Carling, and at other locations on Lake Rosseau as well, and in 1900 they moved their manufacturing operations to the Muskoka Wharf at Gravenhurst. The Muskoka Wharf was the spot where most visitors to Muskoka disembarked from the train and boarded the steamers that took them to the resorts. Arriving at the Wharf meant the holiday had really begun, and as the steamers pulled away from the Wharf on the last leg of a long journey, the happy travellers got a good look at the Ditchburn boatworks. No doubt those moments created many positive associations for an entire generation of cottagers, which certainly didn't hurt the company's image.

The Ditchburn operations quickly prospered and by 1907, Herbert Ditchburn, the son of the hotel clerk brother, had taken over the boat building operation from his uncle, Henry. When the company was incorporated that year, Herb was president, and the directors were his brother Alfred and a key employee named Tom Greavette. Under Herb Ditchburn's guidance, the company grew at a phenomenal pace.

At a 21st century show of antique boats, where Ditchburns bob in the water alongside a dozen other Muskoka marques, it is tempting to view Ditchburn as perhaps the first among equals. But in truth, there was no equal to the success of Ditchburn. It may have been dwarfed by some of the large American manufacturers, with their production line operations, but in Canada the company was to become the dominant builders of pleasure craft. A skilled designer himself, Herb Ditchburn wasn't afraid to employ others whose skills equaled or exceeded his own. His firm also trained hundreds of local men, and changed them from cottage carpenters to polished craftsmen whose workmanship was among the best in the world.

The company was renowned for its fast boats thanks to an association with Commodore Harry Greening, one of the most innovative and respected international boat racers of his generation who drove Ditchburn boats while shattering record after record. It was an approach that is followed to this day by car manufacturers: work with the world's best drivers to design and race cars on the tracks of Indianapolis or Le Mans and use the prestige of winning those races to attract customers. The technological advances developed for the race vehicles are then used to improve the luxurious vehicles made for regular customers.

At the same time, Ditchburn also charted another course that has been used by marketing forces for centuries, selling to the super-rich in the hopes that the merely wealthy will follow in their path. Ditchburn's luxurious and superbly-built boats were purchased by the wealthy and powerful Muskoka cottage owners, like the Eatons and General Motors scion George McLaughlin, and by the 1920s they were also receiving orders from noted clients across North America. A hundred-foot yacht for the commodore of the Royal Canadian Yacht Club, a 66-foot cruiser for the president of Canada Dry Ginger Ale, a 65-foot schooner for distillery magnate Norman Gooderham, and hundreds of others. The Gravenhurst plant was expanded, and expanded again, and a second plant was opened in Orillia, as the orders poured in.

For all the firm's flexibility, for all its ability to build everything from sailboats and ocean-going yachts to ordinary rowing skiffs, it is the displacement hull launch of the 1920s that remains the iconic Ditchburn boat. Boats like *Lady Jayne* or *Wasan* simply emit an elegance and style that is beyond reproach. They are vessels of their era, unabashedly luxurious, proud and assertive rather than genteel. Every element of these boats is executed with style and flair. The lines are drawn with a fine sense of proportion so that even the largest boat looks properly put-together, and the workmanship is simply impeccable. There are many boats out there which have been given names that begin with the word *Lady*, but few seem to bear the title as well as a Ditchburn displacement launch. It is little wonder that these ladies have been kept and coveted for generations.

At 31 and a half feet long, the *Lady Jayne* is an imposing sight, but there is an elegance, a completeness to the boat that makes her seem exactly the right size, regardless of which angle she's seen from. Built in 1924, she is the epitome of Roaring 20s elegance, a boat that is unmistakably a wealthy person's vessel. Current owner Bill Bartells has spent years trying to track down the original owner, but has made it no farther back than the 1960s when the boat lived on the Ottawa River at Hudson, Quebec. It's possible that the owner then, Mr. H.B. Mackenzie, was the original owner, but even repeat visits to the yacht club at Hudson have yielded few clues.

The more recent history of the boat has been recorded: sold to another owner in Quebec, then to three men in Wisconsin who brought the boat to Lake Geneva, 18 years in a barn awaiting restoration, then a brief return trip to Lake Geneva. In 1997, Bill and Eileen Bartells of Lake Rosseau bought the boat and brought her back to Muskoka to be fully and professionally restored by Ed Skinner of Duke Marine Services in Port Carling. Not surprisingly, hardware had gone missing along the way. To replace it, Skinner borrowed hardware from the *Lady Elgin*, another Ditchburn of similar configuration, and had new pieces cast. The engine is the original 125 horsepower Kermath, and the woodwork is 70 per cent original. Only the name is new—unnamed when she was found in Wisconsin, the boat has been christened in memory of the Bartells's daughter. A crystal angel bow light is also dedicated to her.

Although the boat had no top when she was found, holes in the deck planking indicated there had once been a removable top. At first

Bartells thought it should have had a navy top, a simple but effective Muskoka invention that consists of loose canvas strung on a series of bars. But after studying the position of the deck holes, he and Skinner came to the conclusion that the boat was built with an auto top, a retractable top similar to those used on the elegant convertibles of the 1920s. In fact, it seems that Ditchburn built their auto tops using the same hardware as the car companies — there are bolt holes in the hardware that simply aren't needed on a boat, but which may have come in handy on a Cadillac or Buick. Regardless of its origin, though, the auto top looks perfectly at home on the *Lady Jayne*, one more perfect element of a perfect boat.

The same completeness that makes *Lady Jayne* look right is also seen in the *Wasan*. Built three years later than the *Lady Jayne*, and at 27 feet considerably smaller, the *Wasan* is another example of the elegant displacement-hulled launches that have been treasured for decades. Built for the Bishop family of Wasan Island on Lake Rosseau, the boat served faithfully there until the 1950s.

The boom years after the First World War were heady times for wooden boat builders like Ditchburn; the boom years after the second war, however, were not. Fibreglass was the newly favoured material, and even the most elegant wooden boats were going out of fashion.

Dunford had some ideas about how he would paint the gorgeous Ditchburn, Lady Jayne, but all those ideas were abandoned when he saw this image appear. He was standing in the boathouse waiting for the boat to arrive, and caught a glimpse of it through the boathouse window. The scene perfectly captures the relationship between the boat and its environment — boathouses that feature impeccable details like this ornate window, but which are also functional spaces built with knotty wood on the walls. The slightly off-centre view out the window gives the painting a subtle tension and sense of movement.

"A painting like this is all about positive and negative form, about contrast. When I saw that photograph, it just jumped out at me," says Dunford. The artist's job involves finding the elements of the subject that will make a painting complete, that will tell the story that needs to be told. Sometimes the story can be told more effectively by focusing on a detail of a boat like Wasan *rather than looking at the entire boat.*

Fortunately, there were still a number of people around who loved the old wooden boats. Among them were Ralph Boothby and his brother-in-law Glen Coates. The two men were partners in business, having co-founded Fowler Construction in the 1940s. As the firm grew from a small road-building firm that specialized in roads for the logging industry, they decided the time had come to purchase a boat. They'd grown up seeing Ditchburns grace the water, and the two men had no hesitation about buying *Wasan*. They used it as a workboat, storing it in a boathouse beside a sawmill on the Muskoka River, where the docks in Bracebridge's Annie Williams Park now sit. They took the *Wasan* whenever they needed to get to a water-access job site, but the real joy of owning the boat, the real impact on the lives of their families, came on the weekends. "Every Sunday was Riding in The *Wasan* day," Ralph Boothby's daughter Sally recalls. Her father and uncle, their wives and children would all pile into the boat and go for a cruise, the children perched in the mother-in-law seat at the bow, munching chips and drinking orange pop. They might go up to Lake Rosseau for a picnic at a favourite spot, or meet up with other friends in the middle of the lake. In the 1960s Ralph sold his half of the boat to Glen and purchased his own wooden boat, but still the teenaged children went for cruises in the *Wasan*. It was a family cruise boat, and a party boat in the days when it wasn't illegal to spend an evening cruising in the moonlight, singing and sharing a drink with friends as the big engine rumbled beneath the mahogany hatch. It was a boat that was treasured, not because it was a valuable piece of marine heritage, but because it was a beautiful, lovable, functional boat, a pleasure to drive and a joy to behold.

That same undying appeal captured the imagination of Bob Breadner, who now owns the *Wasan*. He'd always loved the elegant Ditchburn launches, and hoped one day to own one. But there aren't many left, and he wasn't sure when he'd get the chance. His opportunity came in 1998. Breadner had just finished building his new cottage on St. Leonard's Island, just a few hundred metres from Wasan Island. With construction completed, Breadner said he wasn't going to spend another penny for quite some time. "I was so sick of writing cheques," he said. A few months later, a friend sent him a picture of *Wasan* and told him it was for sale. Breadner knew such opportunities didn't come along often, and it didn't matter that he had been spending money on a new cottage. If he wanted a Ditchburn launch, he needed to act. His email in reply was brief: "Bastard. How much?"

In the 1920s, when *Wasan* and *Lady Jayne* were built, it seemed as though there were no limits to the potential for the Ditchburn boatworks. Orders poured in from around the world, and the company had an unbeatable reputation for building superb boats. Their designs were superb, and the workmanship was among the best in the world. But in the 1930s, the juggernaut came crashing off course. It was derailed by the departure of Tom Greavette who left to start his own boat company, coupled with ill-timed expansion just as the Great Depression was drying up demand for the luxurious boats that were the firm's mainstay. The company limped through a couple of resurrection attempts before finally closing its doors in 1938.

Herb Ditchburn moved to Trenton, where he began building boats to aid the war effort — fast, 80-foot rescue boats for service in the English Channel, and then steel-hulled harbour tugs for use by the Royal Navy. He died in Trenton in 1950. During his lifetime, Herb Ditchburn built well over 1,000 boats. Most are long-since vanished, but those that remain have taken on a new life. They are the treasures now, and they will remain in cherished service as long as there is water to float them on and people to care for them.

Painting a boat from this perspective brings unique challenges. Looking down on a boat like Llansakes creates a dramatic foreshortening in the sides, forcing the artist to rethink the shape in order to capture the lines of the boat accurately.

5 Fine Work from a Small Shop

As the sun rose higher, a beam of light entered Julius Borneman's workshop on the shores of Gull Lake. He frowned slightly as the light illuminated the dust specks dancing in the air, the last thing he wanted to see as he put the final coat of varnish on his latest boat. He'd been varnishing since first light, making the most of the lack of dust in the early morning air, and he hoped the final coat would soon be dry.

This much varnish on a boat didn't seem right to his eye. Perhaps he was old-fashioned, but he preferred the traditional look, a cypress hull painted white, with varnish limited to the topsides and interiors. But the Miller family had wanted the entire boat built of mahogany and varnished, and customers had to be catered to. Particularly customers who lived on a grand estate up on Lake Rosseau. Particularly customers who were buying boats so soon after the war.

The Great War hadn't been kind to Julius, his younger brother, Herman, and their cousin Abe Wishman who worked alongside him in the boatshop. Most of their neighbours in Gravenhurst remained as friendly as they always had been, recognizing that the Bornemans, the Wishmans and other German families had been born and raised in Canada and had no love for the Kaiser and his army. But there had been a few mutterings against them and the other families from Germania, the hamlet a few miles outside town where Julius's grandparents had staked out their farm in the 1880s. And as the death tolls from Europe rose higher, the voices grew louder.

Still, the war years had been boom years in Muskoka, particularly in the years before America entered the war — travel to Europe was impossible, so more Americans chose to come north for their holidays — and boat builders across the district had been busy. Over on the other side of town, Herb Ditchburn was doing so well that he'd built a new, brick factory in 1915 when the old wooden shop burned down.

Julius had changed locations too, moving a few yards inland in 1914 to turn the town's old power plant into a boatworks. He and his brother had been on Gull Lake since 1908 when they built a two-storey boat livery at the foot of Brock Street. It was a good location from which to rent canoes and rowboats, and even with a competing livery right next door their business had thrived. In the summer as many as two dozen canoes and rowing skiffs bobbed at the dock in front of the workshop, waiting for local residents and summer tourists to rent one for a few hours of fun. When the lake froze over and the tourists went home, the brothers built more canoes and rowboats.

They learned the skills from other boat builders in the area and by copying other boats they'd seen. They were meticulous workers with a good understanding of how a boat should come together, and it wasn't long before people started asking them to apply their skills to build something larger, to build a motor launch just like those Mr. Ditchburn was producing.

The Bornemans were happy to oblige. One of their first boats was a slim, 18-footer built for Pete Kohn. Not even wide enough for two people to sit side-by-side, equipped with a small motor mounted on the floor and a rope tiller for steering, it slipped quickly through the water, bringing envious glances from the rowers and paddlers. That same year, 1909, they built something a bit more ambitious, a 23-foot motor launch named *Ruth*. They had no way of knowing it would be one of the few boats of theirs that would survive into the next century.

To build these ever-larger and more complex launches, the Bornemans simply did what they'd always done, what most of the small builders around the lakes did: they studied what others were building, copied what they liked and innovated a way around features they didn't care for. Nobody seemed to worry about copyrighting a hull shape, and above-the-waterline design elements were varied enough that each builder retained his own unique look, even if the distinctions were subtle. Since Ditchburn was the largest boat builder in town, it wasn't surprising that Julius and Herman mimicked his designs. The early motor launches from both shops had a pronounced deck crown that was carried through to both the oversized engine hatches and the arched windshields. But this was 1919, and styles had changed. The boat Julius was finishing had a more subtle deck crown and an upward sweep to the deck just before the windshield, and the windshield itself was square rather than arched, just like those being built by Herb Ditchburn. Some of the interior elements, like the carved curlicue on the arms of the rear seat, also evoked touches used by Ditchburn and others.

Stepping back to study his handiwork, Julius's gaze lingered over the transom. This was the part of the boat he had always liked best, a complex series of curves that gave the boat its character. It wasn't easy to build a boat that looked good and performed well, and the lines of the transom had an impact on both aspects of the boat's design. Some of his favourite boats had an extreme curvature at the transom, coupled with a pronounced set of "hips" that made the boat look pretty and ride well. He recalled the *Torpitt*, the launch he'd built for Torpitt Lodge on Sparrow Lake. It was a big boat meant to carry guests and their luggage from the train station to the lodge, and he smiled as he recalled a photograph someone had taken of the boat on regatta day. The boat wasn't riding quite right in the water in that picture, which was hardly surprising given what it was carrying and towing. Packed with at least 15 passengers, it was towing a long line of rowboats down the lake, each of them filled with smiling guests. The boat immediately behind *Torpitt* was even more heavily laden, its gunwales mere inches above the water as an entire brass band stood and played a salute.

Chuckling at the thought, Julius applied the last lick of varnish, sealed the can, then sauntered outside to enjoy the feel of the rising sun. It was a good boat; it was going to be a good year.

⊕ ⊕ ⊕

In the early years of the last century, there were numerous small builders like the Bornemans plying their trade around the lakes. The brothers were unique in a couple of respects, though. For one thing, they built even their largest boats in canoe fashion, bending steamed ribs around a mold and planking the boat upside down, rather than building the boat rightside up on heavy wooden frames. The resulting boats were light, but also had a more rounded bottom and tended to roll a bit in a cross wind.

The other thing that made the Bornemans unique is that they didn't stay in the boat business. Many builders had the craft in their blood. Even though they could make more money building homes and cottages, they kept coming back to the boat work they loved. The Bornemans, though, moved on to other things. In the mid-twenties, likely facing increased competition from larger builders like Herb Ditchburn, they closed their boat shop and opened a Ford dealership and garage. In 1937, wanting a business his children could take over, Julius sold the garage and opened Gravenhurst's first movie theatre. It still stands on the town's main street although it stopped showing movies years ago.

But even though the Borneman family moved away from boat building, a handful of the vessels they crafted continued to ply the local waters. The *Llansakes*, which Julius and Herman built for the Miller family of Llanllar estate, remained with the family until 1957 when Mrs. Miller traded it in on a new Greavette. A cottager named Bob Purves was at the Greavette plant when the boat arrived and bought it on sight, paying $1,800 for it. He stored it in a friend's boathouse for two years until he could get his own boathouse built, and later passed it on to his son Robert Purves.

The *Llansakes* is one of only three Bornemans known to exist today. Even Julius Borneman didn't have one of his own boats: when he died in 1947 he owned a Greavette, which he looked after with meticulous and loving care.

Long deck launches and canoes are both old-fashioned boats, but they are still actively used in Muskoka. This painting was conceived as a way of showing that both kinds of boats still share the waterways. The brightly-painted canvas canoes flanking the rich wood of the cedar strip canoe, the pile of firewood stacked between two hemlock trees, and the launch cruising sedately past all add up to a statement about the way various users share the landscape.

6

The Ubiquitous Canoe

A true Canadian," Pierre Berton wrote, "is someone who can make love in a canoe without tipping." Any canoeists who have tried to prove their national identity soon discover that the problem is not only one of balance but also one of thwarts, seats and yoke, but Berton's point is well taken. There are probably as many canoes in Canadian homes, camps and cottages as there are all other forms of boats combined. Nearly every boathouse has at least one, and there are many homes that have a canoe and nothing else. No boat shape in Canada is as immediately recognized as the canoe. It is a part of our collective culture, a part of our self-definition.

Yet there is a paradox at work here: we may claim to treasure these boats, yet ignorance about them has never been greater. Ask a boat owner about his fleet, and he will be able to tell you the year, size and builder of every powerboat he has ever owned; ask about his canoes, though, and you will likely get a blank look. Canoes are stocked in every Wal-Mart and Canadian Tire store, where they are sold by the foot like 2x4 lumber. Looking for a solo canoe? You want the 12-foot model. To carry two people and camping gear, you should consider the 16-footer. Design considerations are largely restricted to construction materials — light kevlar if you can afford it, bullet-tough ABS plastic if you're planning to bounce down the rapids, and fibreglass or aluminum as the basic options.

But far from the department stores there is another world of canoe building, a realm where designers still contemplate how much rocker a boat should have, or whether to soften the chines just a little bit more. Creative builders work in all kinds of materials, but par-ticularly in wood. Canoe building remains the most vigorous branch of wooden boat construction, with thousands of builders from professional craftsmen to backyard hobbyists who know how to shape cedar, stretch canvas, and steam bend ash gunwales to create a creature of lasting beauty. Far from mimicking their predecessors, these builders continue to refine designs and modify construction methods. There is a vitality in their work, a realization that, even though the basic design has been around for centuries, an individual canoe can still be perfectly matched to an individual paddler.

Canoe building remains vital and vibrant, but for creative designing no era can match the few decades of the late 19th century when canoe construction went from being a craft to an industry. One of the first developments came in Peterborough, a bustling town located where the deep soiled farmland of the Great Lakes-St. Lawrence Lowland gives way to the rugged hills and cold lakes of the Canadian Shield. Settlers had been coming there since the 1820s, and soon discovered what settlers across eastern North America realized, that canoes were essential tools in a region with many rivers and few roads. At first they bought birchbark canoes from their neighbours, the Algonquin and Ojibwa natives who had been building these canoes for hundreds of years. Then the settlers learned to make dugouts. The word conjures images of awkward and ugly shaped logs, but the Peterborough dugouts were works of art. Hard and sharp steel tools allowed the settlers to give elegant shape and form to the basswood and butternut logs they carved. By driving pegs into the outside of the hull as thickness guides, they could make the hulls as little as half an inch thick. With butternut or walnut decks, maple or oak thwarts and outwales of white oak, the dugouts were fast and elegant craft.

But even with steel tools, carving a dugout was an enormous amount of work, and by the 1850s innovative builders began to invent ways of building a canoe using wooden planks. A blacksmith and woodworker named John Stephenson and a young boat builder named Tom Gordon were the first to think of using a dugout canoe as a mold. In 1857 they steamed and bent oak ribs over the outside of the dugout, then used hot water to bend 1/4 inch thick basswood planks over the ribs. They had invented the wide board canoe, and by 1861 the canoe was being produced and sold. Over the next few decades, other builders in Peterborough and nearby towns like Lakefield modified this design. They created the double cedar canoe, with two layers of thin planking and a sheet of waterproofed canvas sandwiched in between; there was the cedar rib canoe, with tongue and groove planks running gunwale to gunwale rather than the length of the boat; and there were other variations.

In Maine, meanwhile, the industry was taking a different direction. Settlers there had learned to build birchbark canoes, and had turned it into an industry. As the supply of large birch trees dwindled, they discovered that canvas could take its place, and in the 1870s the cedar canvas canoe was born. Before long these two styles of canoe building, the all-wood canoes of Peterborough and the cedar canvas canoes of Maine, would battle for dominance, each claiming a share of a growing market as canoeing grew in popularity.

And grow it did. There were still a few frontier regions in eastern North America at that time, but an increasing number of people were working far away from the fields and forests so familiar a few generations earlier. They worked in office buildings and factories, lived in cities where the coal smoke and industrial fumes hung thick in the air. When they managed to get a few hours away from work, they wanted to get out and enjoy fresh air, clean water and sunshine. They wanted to get out in a canoe. They rented them by the hour in any city with a lake or a river running through it. They cheered on canoe racers and bought boats by the builders who made the fastest canoes — Walter Dean of Toronto was renowned for his fast boats, and advertised them with slogans like 'Deans' Canoes MUST paddle easy for they ALWAYS WIN.' They soaked up books by outdoor writers like George Washington Sears (known as Nessmuk), and planned canoe trips inspired by his exploits.

With its numerous lakes and rivers and its proximity to Toronto, Muskoka could have been ideally suited to capitalize on the canoe-building boom. But, in one of those historical accidents that determine boat building trends, the region largely missed out on canoes. People in Muskoka needed boats just as much as Peterborough's early residents, but settlers didn't begin to arrive in Muskoka in large numbers until the 1860s, around the time the first wide board canoes were rolling out of the shops in Peterborough. While boat builders in Peterborough and Maine were building factories and organizing production lines, Muskoka's settlers were still rowing logs to the nearest sawmill to have them cut into lumber, and campaigning to have the railway extended into the district. A few boat builders tried to make a living with canoes, but most soon realized they couldn't compete with the cheaper product coming by rail from Peterborough, and later from the Chestnut factory in New Brunswick. Some builders like Ditchburn stopped crafting their own canoes, and instead bought canoes from Peterborough and put their own name plate on them. They could then sell canoes to any customers who wanted one, while focusing their attention on the more lucrative business of building motor launches.

But even though most of them weren't built locally, canoes

Summer Dreams *is Doug Dunford's tribute to the power that boats have to carry us anywhere we desire.*
He has painted this scene before, in a slightly different painting called Summer Dreamer.

quickly became an essential part of life in Muskoka. Settlers needed canoes to get to town or to hunt the deer and ducks that helped them survive the winter, while vacationers just wanted to get out on the water. Rowing skiffs were perfect for the big lakes, but for travelling along a river or hopping between small lakes, there was still nothing to rival a canoe.

In fact, Muskoka's first vacation incarnation had more to do with canoe camping than cottaging. While luxurious resorts soon sprang up, Muskoka was also renowned as a place where weary urbanites could find refreshment through a week or two of paddling and sleeping in tents, just as they do now in Algonquin Park. If a 19th century resident of Toronto told his friends he was going to "canoe country," he usually meant Muskoka. Well into the 20th century it was possible to find a campsite along the shores of any lake or river in Muskoka, and established canoe routes soon developed. Trips to and from Georgian Bay were popular, both with short-term visitors and with cottagers who used a canoe trip to break up the month or two they were spending at the cottage. Portages and even excavated channels called canoe cuts were developed — paddlers could avoid the rapids on the Joe River, for example, by using a 250-yard portage at Cumberland Bay to get from Lake Joseph to Lake Rosseau. It was the post-war boom of the 1920s that killed canoe camping in Muskoka. The strong economy and ease of transportation provided by better cars brought a flurry of building to the area. Favourite camping spots were soon walled off by new cottages, and old canoe routes had to be rethought. As the number of paddlers declined, the old portages began to grow over, and some landowners even had the temerity to post No Trespassing signs at rapids and waterfalls where the portages had been used for millennia.

The motor, meanwhile, was beginning to change canoe design. Better motors were making motorboats more reliable, so canoes were no longer necessary as a way of getting to church or going for groceries. As people paddled less, their skills stagnated so that it was more work to paddle when they did go out. A three-mile trip down the lake no longer seemed inconsequential; it seemed like work. People still wanted to have canoes at the cottage, though, so canoe builders kept producing them. But slowly, over the course of decades, they modified their designs. Their customers weren't as skilled, so the canoes had to be a bit squatter to accommodate paddlers who were less adept at keeping their balance. People who didn't paddle every day could no longer recognize the differences a high bow or a pronounced tumblehome could have on a boat's performance. The canoe market split into two distinct groups: some buyers just wanted a cheap boat to fool around in, while others understood and appreciated the subtleties of design and construction that make a boat truly special. The people who built canoes in Muskoka — and there have always been a few, working from small shops scattered around the district — largely concentrated on the latter market, crafting vessels which are a delight to paddle as well as to look at.

For all its ups and downs, the canoe still has power and appeal, even to those who buy their boats at a department store. They are often the first boats children are allowed to control, the boats a land-loving guest will happily take out for an afternoon. And there remains no other vessel that so completely conforms itself to the body of the user, a boat which, when it is well designed and well built, seems to respond not only to one's actions but to one's thoughts. A skilled paddler in the right boat is not just a boat operator, she is an aquatic creature, a river-borne mermaid travelling with an artistry and a grace that is evident to all. The paddle is an extension of her arm, the boat an extension of her body, and nothing would be easier for her than to make love on the water.

7   Powered by Wind and Oar

They were the minivans of the waterways, seen everywhere carrying people, luggage, firewood and food. Settlers used them to go to church on Sunday and to tow booms of logs to the sawmills. Tourists used them for fishing and social visits, for moonlight cruises and for quiet trysts.

Even more surprising than the ubiquity of rowboats was the similarity of their design. When motorboats came on the scene, enthusiasts could easily tell a Ditchburn from a Minett, and a Walter Dean canoe wasn't difficult to pick out in a crowd of Peterboroughs and Old Towns. But even though there were dozens of builders in Muskoka and Georgian Bay producing rowboats, with a few exceptions their work is very difficult to tell apart. A Muskoka skiff is a very different boat from the rowboats built on the St. Lawrence River or in the Ottawa Valley, but the differences between a Duke from Port Carling and a Gravenhurst-built Ditchburn evade the casual glance.

The typical Muskoka rowing skiff is 15 or 16 feet long, and 46 inches wide. The ribs and gunwales are white oak, with five or six white cedar planks on each side, nailed together in lapstrake fashion. They are double-ended, with "fine" lines at either end. There are a few differences that help experts to tell one boat from another — Georgian Bay boats tended to have a bit more freeboard than Muskoka boats, and individual builders attached the seats to the hull in different ways, or had slight variations in the way they finished the area at the points of each boat. But for the most part the builders simply copied what their peers were doing, constructing boats that were easy to build and functional to use.

Few builders poured their passion into rowboat design. They just knew that the basic design worked, and worked well. The lapstrake construction wasn't just easy for the builders, it helped break up the waves and kept the water from splashing into the boat. The fine points at either end gave the boats forward momentum that kept them from slowing down between each stroke. The length and beam created a boat that was stable and seaworthy, and fast enough to get rowers to their destination in time.

The differences between them are subtle when they're tied up at the dock, but they are apparent to anyone who rows a lot of them. George Rossiter has restored hundreds of rowboats, and has tested most of them. "I would get them all refinished and varnished and looking beautiful and I would take them out to test them," he said. "I'd wait until it was a windy day, and I was amazed at how different they were. Some would row beautifully and track nicely and go across the wind, and others were just monsters."

Armed with a degree in marine architecture, Rossiter set about trying to understand what made the difference between the beauties and the beasts, and using that knowledge to build his own rowboats. He measured the angles of the hull — half angle of entry, half angle of exit, deadrise, and so on — and found that the varying measurements accounted for some of the difference in performance. He saw that the oars could clear the wave tops more effectively on boats with vertical planks at the sheerline, and that the lapstrake hulls seemed to move faster than the occasional smoothskin hull he came across, as though the laps were trapping air under the water.

Sailboats have a strange place in the heart: they are loved by their owners but also by people who have no desire to sail. Wooden sailboats like this Aykroyd dinghy are almost all gone, but sitting in a Muskoka chair at the end of the dock and watching the sailboats go past remains a popular summer pastime.

Dunford starting painting Muskoka chairs in the 1970s, and his paintings became so popular that he spawned numerous imitators. "I loved painting those old chairs. Each one has its own personality," he said. "At one time I said 'I'm not going to do this any more because everyone is doing it.' Then I decided I didn't care what everyone else is doing." The launch entering from the left is the Marco.

He also discovered that the beautiful old Muskoka skiffs are not the ideal boats for modern rowers. A good rowboat must fit the rower, so that he is pulling the oars into his chest rather than into his shoulders or lap. The foot blocks need to be in the right spot, the seat needs to be at the right height, and all of it needs to be centred in such a way that the boat stays level as the rower leans forward and back. And as he measured and calculated, Rossiter realized that the old Muskoka rowboats were designed to fit old Muskoka rowers, people who lived in an era when a six-foot man was considered to be tall. "The traditional boat is good for somebody five foot eight," he said. "If they're longer or shorter, they're really not going to be that comfortable."

Modern boats like Rossiter's take into account the size of modern rowers. They also include elements like adjustable sliding seats, things which were seen in racing sculls a century ago, but rarely used in traditional rowboats.

But it wasn't the changing size of rowers that led owners to pull their rowboats into the woods to rot, or scuttle them in the bay. It was the advent of power, the invention of the marine engine that suddenly made rowing even the best boat seem like a lot more work. When boaters were given the choice between rowing to town and riding to town, it wasn't long before the rowboats were banished to the back of the boathouse.

It was natural that motors would make oars irrelevant, for they were an extension of the ancient human ambition to cover more distance with less effort. People had already been doing the same thing with sails, raising a mast in the centre of the rowboat, attaching a boom and a sail, and sailing down the lake. These modified skiffs would sail all right, but the hull design wasn't right and the boats were notoriously unstable — "a deathtrap for the unskilled," in the words of Toronto Telegram editor C.H.J. Snider, "which would capsize with the weight of its own sail."

Novice sailors in Toronto could rent these boats for 10 cents per half hour in the 1880s, and venture out for a day of sailing on the clear waters of the harbour. George Aykroyd and his father Henry rented out plenty of these boats from their livery at the foot of York Street, and just like the Muskoka livery owners who were renting boats a hundred miles to the north, the Aykroyds spent their winters building new boats. They soon realized, though, that they needed something better than a converted rowboat; they needed a boat that would be quick and easy to build but would have the same attributes under sail as a rowing skiff had when driven by oars — easy to use, and with an idiot-proof stability. In 1898, fellow Torontonian Wilson Morse developed the boat they'd been looking for. He called it a dinghy, drawing for some unknown reason on the Hindi word for small boat, dingi. It was 12 feet long and nearly five feet wide, a full foot wider than the 16-foot rowing skiffs people had been sailing in. With a forward-mounted mast and a centreboard for added stability, it was both fast and stable, easy and fun to sail. It became, yacht designer George Cuthbertson says, "the Laser of its day," beloved by racers and recreational sailors alike.

Morse had designed his dinghy for camping trips amid the islands of Georgian Bay, but the Aykroyds realized the boat would also be perfectly suited to their livery business. They adapted the design to make the boat faster and began building them by the dozen, stocking them in their own rental fleet and selling 14, 16 and 18-foot models. Other builders in Toronto, Muskoka and elsewhere also adopted the design, but few specialized in them the way George Aykroyd did. After his father died, George continued building boats, producing up to 50 a year and shipping them wherever customers could be found. Hundreds went to Muskoka, travelling by rail to Gravenhurst for two dollars a boat, and generations of sailors learned their craft while skipping across the water on an Aykroyd 14.

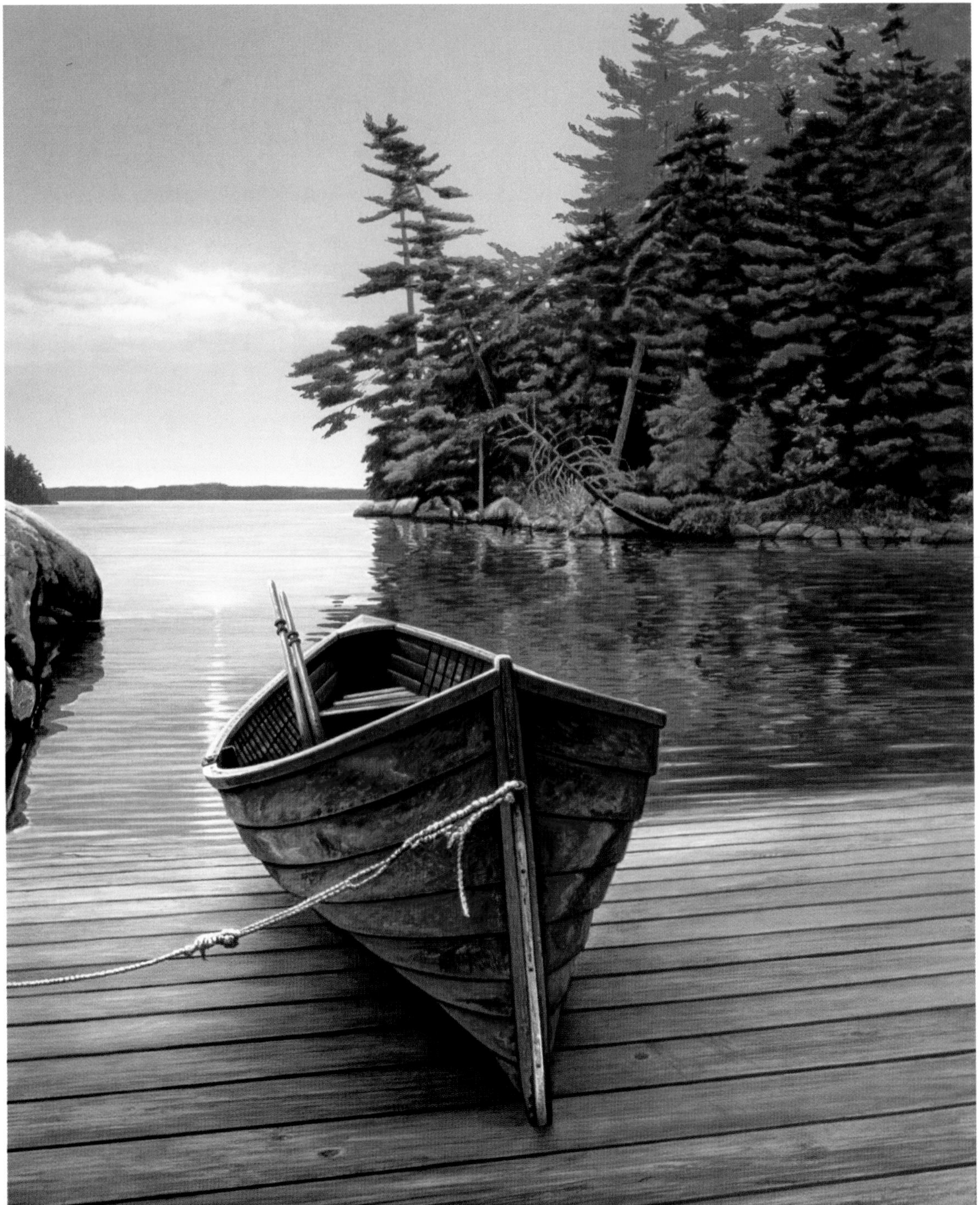
D.K. Dunford

In 1945 George Aykroyd and his longtime assistant John Wells, both in their 80s, launched the 2,500th Aykroyd dinghy, one of the last they would build before finally retiring. Aykroyd dinghies were still popular with recreational sailors and novices — the 2,501st boat was one of three ordered by the Taylor Statten summer camp in Algonquin Park — but the design had long since been supplanted in the racing fraternity. It wasn't long before recreational sailors turned away from wooden dinghies too, embracing new designs and new materials that required less maintenance and allowed more time for sailing.

It would be another 40 years before people began to restore and appreciate the old wooden sailboats again, and in that time the vast majority of Aykroyd's dinghies would vanish. Time and neglect are not kind to wooden boats, and they are particularly hard on wooden sailboats. Unless they had a high-roofed boathouse or enjoyed raising and lowering the mast, many people simply left their sailboats outside all summer where the sun and weather played hard on the varnish and the woodwork beneath it. An unwanted rowing skiff might be tucked away in the back of the boathouse, forgotten for many seasons until the changing fashions of boating inspire someone to restore it and launch it again. The old sailboats were often rendered unsightly in much less time. Hauled into the woods, burned for firewood, or simply scuttled, they have all but vanished.

There are a few left, including a fleet of treasured Aykroyds that races every summer weekend on Stony Lake in the Kawarthas. But for wooden dinghies and rowing skiffs alike, the future lies primarily in the hands of the backyard builder. George Rossiter loves the old wooden boats, but financial reality dictates that he build his modern rowboats from fibreglass. There are simply not many people willing to pay a professional builder $8,000 to craft a new wooden skiff or dinghy. But in the home builder's workshop, where time is not money, wood remains the ideal building material — flexible, forgivable, and a pleasure to work with. The designs that were refined by George Aykroyd and the hundreds of anonymous skiff builders a century ago are still passed around among amateur builders, and every spring, as the ice disappears from the lakes and another boating season begins, another set of garage doors opens and a new wooden skiff or dinghy prepares to begin a life of service on the water.

AT LEFT: *"This boat and Governor's Island are one," said Dunford. "There's no separating the two. The boat is as much a part of it as the trees and the rocks." The island and the skiff were both once owned by a painter who often rowed around the island on sketching cruises. The painting shows the boat waiting patiently for another artist or visitor to go on a similar trip.*

There's no finer place to see Muskoka's wooden boat treasures than at the annual boat show at Muskoka Wharf in Gravenhurst.
The Segwun is always a part of the show, grace meeting speed as the dignified old steamship berths alongside the beautiful mahogany racers and launches.

8   The Romance of Steam

The love of old boats is a romantic passion; the love of old steamboats is much more than that. "It's an obsessive-compulsive disorder," says Jerry Hamlin. "For those who are into it, it's like a disease." By implication, those who are not into it are forever outside the realm, destined to never understand it.

Hamlin was quite young when he made his first forays into the quirky subculture of steamboating. He watched Humphrey Bogart pilot a steamboat in *The African Queen*, then watched antique cars race in the movie *Genevieve*, and the two films combined into a resolve to one day own a steam car. He later realized that steam cars are really not practical unless you have a large estate with private roads on which they can be driven. "We didn't have one of those. But we did have an island."

He tinkered with boats for years — one of his more memorable experiments was a sailboat which he converted to a paddle wheeler, powered by a Rider-Ericsson hot air engine that had formerly powered the water pump at his family's cottage.

In 1967 he bought his first steamboat and brought it to the family cottage on Lake Joseph's Cliff Island. It was a step, but it wasn't exactly the boat he was looking for. The one he wanted belonged to Norman Hatherley at Lake Joseph's Gordon Bay Marina. Twenty-five feet long and five foot two inches wide, it had unusual lines with a bow that angled slightly forward into the water like a First World War frigate, and Hamlin had fallen in love with it as soon as he saw it. Hatherley had converted the old steamboat to gas and used it regularly.

After Hatherley died, Hamlin offered to buy the boat from his estate. The executors made Hamlin another offer: they would give him the boat, along with the original engine and boiler, if he agreed to restore it. Hamlin accepted, throwing in fifty dollars for a basket full of brass fittings to complete the boat, and in 1970 the restoration project began.

It would take him nearly 20 years to get the boat back on the water. "It takes *years* to put a steamboat together," he said. "You have to find everything." He soon decided the engine and boiler would both need to be replaced — the engine wasn't a particularly good one to begin with, and the boiler just looked unsafe. But the first thing anyone restoring a steamboat needs to do is to find the people who know what parts you need and how to put them together. Hamlin toured the lakes, interviewing anyone who could tell him about old steamboats, or about his steamboat in particular. He tracked down machinists and engineers who had parts in their sheds and garages, and who could help him fit the pieces together.

Along the way, he encountered others who had been bitten by the same steam bug. There was a retired engineer in St. Catharines who had learned to love steam while working on the Great Lakes — even today there are lake freighters that use steam engines, burning a thick, tar-like bunker oil to heat the water in their massive boilers, then capturing the steam power to turn the enormous screws. A part-time machinist with a love of steam power, the man had cast three replicas of a 1902 Mills Compound engine as a retirement project, and sold one to Hamlin.

Turning the rough casting into a usable engine took another year of work, this time by a Bracebridge-based engineer named Roy Davies. "Roy is a genius," Hamlin said. Not only did he get the engine running, but Davies built a new boiler from scratch.

There were a handful of other steam-lovers on the lakes as well. There are now five steam-powered yachts like Hamlin's that still use the old form of propulsion, and some of their owners were engaged in restorations around the same time. But in the 1970s the most active group of steam fans were found at the other end of Muskoka, trying desperately to get the last of the large steamers back in operation on the lakes.

The R.M.S. *Segwun* is now an icon of Muskoka, the oldest boat on the lakes and an essential part of summer. But in the early 1970s it was slowly rotting away, changing from a ship to a hulk. The hull had been in service since 1887, when it was launched as a paddle wheeler named the *Nipissing*. In the 1920s it was overhauled, turned into a stern-drive ship, and renamed the *Segwun*, an Ojibwe word meaning 'springtime.'

The *Segwun* was once part of a large and vibrant fleet of steamships, the lifelines that connected communities around the lakes. They ferried passengers to and from the resorts, carried mail and supplies, and even towed booms of logs to the sawmills and barges piled high with hemlock bark to the tanneries. They employed dozens of people directly, and supplied the industries that kept hundreds more working. Before the roads were built, and even before the railway reached past Gravenhurst, it was the steamers that made life in Muskoka possible.

By the 1950s, though, steamship travel had become an anachronism. Improved roads and better vehicles made travel by boat completely unnecessary; the dwindling fortunes of the company that owned the boats had resulted in some poor maintenance, so the boats were too shabby and sad-looking to be desirable as cruising vessels for tourists. One by one, the old steamers were sidelined — burned or scuttled, sold for scrap or simply left to rot. In 1958 the grand old *Sagamo*, once the flagship of the Muskoka Lakes fleet, was the last of the steamers to make a commercial run. Soon it and the *Segwun* were the last survivors, desolate old ladies neglected at the side of the dock in Gravenhurst. The *Sagamo* served a season as a restaurant, and another as a nightclub. It was even being spruced up for another season when a heater used to warm some paint caught fire, igniting a blaze that soon engulfed the grand old ship. In 1969, the *Segwun* alone remained.

Afraid they would lose the last tangible reminder of the steamboat era, Muskoka residents raised funds to turn the *Segwun* into a floating museum. But gradually another idea began to take hold, first among a handful of steam enthusiasts, then slowly among an ever-growing group of people. What if the old steamship could sail again? What if the chuff of the steam engine wasn't silenced forever?

The hurdles were enormous, and very similar to the ones being faced by Jerry Hamlin, Paul Dodington, Paul Gockel and all the other steamboat-lovers who were restoring their own whimsical dream boats. People with expertise needed to be found, and machinery needed to be replaced or rebuilt. The labyrinthine shoals of the commercial shipping regulations needed to be navigated in order to find a way for the old boat to carry passengers once again. But as slowly as pressure rising in a steam boiler, obstacle after obstacle gave way.

In the early 1970s the dream of relaunching the *Segwun* ceased to be a hope and instead became a goal. Former engineers provided

Some boats have a relationship with a particular person, and that's certainly the case with Wendigo. The connection between the boat and Jerry Hamlin, the man who spent years restoring it, is so profound that Dunford couldn't imagine painting the boat without its owner at the helm.

their expertise, cottagers and residents who had served or sailed on the old ship donated funds and lobbied for more. The Ontario Roadbuilders Association provided key funding — the group said the good roads its members had built had helped render steamboats obsolete, so it made sense for its members to get involved in preserving the last of the steamships; it didn't hurt that several key members of the group were Muskoka residents, including two of the association's former presidents who still used a Ditchburn launch as a workboat. Even with all that help, it took years before the ship was finally able to sail again, but on June 21, 1981, the familiar deep 'whooooop' of the whistle sounded once more and the ship embarked on the third maiden voyage of its career.

The image of the *Segwun* has become a symbol of Muskoka, its familiar white superstructure and black and red smokestack appearing in every magazine article and tourist brochure. But one can't really understand the appeal of a steamboat from on shore — you need to venture aboard and go below decks. It's only there, amid the hissing machinery, that you can get a glimpse of the mechanism that has inspired such passion. There is noise there, but it is a different order of noise than is found in an internal combustion engine room. There is oil in the air, but it is the gentle scent of lubricating oil rather than the acrid whiff of combustion, a scent that teases your nostrils rather than assaulting them. It is in the engine room that the soul of this ship is found, a hissing, clanking siren song that calls its lovers to go to extraordinary lengths. Steam is the engine of the undying romantic.

In 1989, Jerry Hamlin's boat was completed. During the course of his restorations, he had learned something of the boat's history. Built in Torrance on Lake Muskoka, likely around 1889, it had been named the *Pickerel*, and later the *Opechee*, which means 'robin'. Like most of the small steamboats, it had been a working boat, designed to pull log booms or barges, or deliver supplies to the areas the large ships like the *Nipissing* didn't serve. Hamlin was the first owner to view it as a recreational craft, the first to fit it out with the sort of detailed woodwork that, in the 1890s would have been reserved for the larger steam yachts owned by wealthy cottagers like the Eatons.

He renamed the boat *Wendigo*, after the native spirit that haunts travellers in the woods. And slowly he began to learn how to operate this creature he had brought back to life. Hamlin invited some of the old steam hands to travel with him, to take the controls and work the boat as they had done when they were young. Hamlin studied their movements, and noticed a difference from his own. When he was running the boat, Hamlin was constantly moving, checking the water pressure, ensuring the water pump was still running, feeding the fire, and tinkering. "I noticed that the old-timers who operated my boat were like Yoda. They'd move very slowly."

They'd put some wood in the firebox, then sit for a minute. Check the water pump, then sit for a minute.

Engineers aboard the *Segwun* do the same thing, spending as much time listening to the engine as they do looking at the gauges or making adjustments. As he spent more time on board his own boat, Hamlin began to learn the engine's rhythm, to hear the music of its song. "Then you get into the steam Zen zone," he said.

That "steam Zen zone" has taken Hamlin throughout the contiguous Muskoka lakes, and — with the recent addition of a trailer and a towing vehicle — on "Steam Treks" to Skeleton Lake and the chain of three lakes in Huntsville. Hamlin is considering towing *Wendigo* south to cruise the waters of Florida, and he'd love to take it all the way to the Amazon. He's been told he could be killed towing a steamboat through some parts of Central America, and the Highway of the Americas that is supposed to connect North and South America is still broken by a 50-mile-gap in the jungles of Panama. But those are mere practical considerations, and in the world of steamboat-lovers, practical considerations are nothing as long as one has vision and romance on one's side.

It's early morning and Our Cup of Tea is tied up at the dock, ready to go for a cruise. The water is an important element of the painting, an environment which is drawing the boat into it. "The darkness behind the boat in the background provides contrast with the light shining on top of the roof," said Dunford. "There's light and dark making the statement that allows the boat to sit out in front of everything."

9   Drawing Rooms on the Water

Our Cup of Tea sits graciously at the dock, the bumpers gently jostling the cypress planks as an early morning swell lifts the boat. Half a dozen Muskoka chairs are arranged in a semi-circle on the dock, as if awaiting an audience that will emerge from the grand old cottage on Lake Muskoka, stroll down to the water's edge and sit to admire this lovely craft.

It's a scene straight out of the 1930s, a moment that is apparently unchanged since the days when wealthy cottagers had their staff bring boats like this to meet them at the train station in Gravenhurst. Appearances are deceiving, for this boat has only been in Muskoka for a few years, but the spirit it captures is one that is familiar to generations of local cottagers. The appeal of cruising slowly along the lake, gazing out the window in any weather, is undying.

Our Cup of Tea was built in Oakville in 1931, commissioned by distillery owner Alex Gooderham who wanted a boat that would keep him and his guests dry as they travelled from the train to their island cottage in Temagami. It was both the first and last of its kind, a custom-designed vessel that was delivered the year the boatworks went bankrupt, and it served the family well for 16 years. The boat then went through a series of owners before ending up in the woods near North Bay, where it was seen by buyers Lloyd and Susan Ross, along with boat restorer Ed Skinner of Duke Boatworks, and boat broker Joe Charles. All four agreed it was a unique boat, unlike any they'd seen before, with lines that suggested a variety of influences including a raised bow that gave the sheerline a vaguely Dutch look. The once-elegant woodwork was covered in layers of paint, and the seating consisted of plywood benches, but Lloyd and Susan Ross could see the beauty that lurked beneath. "I just saw this funny-looking boat," Ed Skinner says. "But it turned out to be the perfect boat for what they wanted it for."

What they wanted it for was quiet, social cruising, puttering along the shoreline with friends. It was perfect for that purpose, as if that was what it had been made for. And in a sense, it had been built for social cruising. The man who commissioned it may have only wanted a means of getting to and from an island, but the boat's design heritage is to be seen in something much more elegant: it is descended from the picnic boats that were popular a generation earlier, and the sailing yachts of the Victorian era. Some boat designs are inextricably linked to the means of propulsion, to advances in hull design, or simply to the fashions of a certain era. But the spirit that infuses cabin launches like *Our Cup of Tea* springs from the purpose of the boats rather than from anything as changeable as mere technology. The details varied over the years, but from the Victorian era to the middle of the next century, whether they were propelled by steam, gas, electricity, or even sail, there is a commonality to be seen in all of the elegant cruisers and yachts, a unifying thread that marks them as sister ships.

Another member of this family is to be found on Lake of Bays on the east side of Muskoka. *Heather Belle* was built in 1902, commissioned by Sidney Finlay Mckinnon of Toronto and Lake Rosseau for use by his daughter, Elizabeth Miles. (1902 was a good year for the Mckinnon family fleet, for that same year Mckinnon launched *Rambler*, another luxurious yacht which is still found in Muskoka.)

The *Heather Belle* was built by the Marine Engine and Machine Company of New Jersey, and was featured prominently in the company's catalogue the next year. The black and white catalogue image of the interior captures the essence of the vessel perfectly, with lush leather upholstery, carved mahogany woodwork, and a modern linoleum floor. Perhaps most striking, though, and most revealing about the fashion of the day, are the windows. In the drawing that appeared in the company's catalogue, the windows are blank, with no indication of what sort of scenery might be seen outside the vessel. They are heavily "dressed," with rich, tasseled drapes pulled back and tied to the frames with satin cords. Similar drapes hang at the ends of the two benches. What results is an image almost entirely lacking in marine references. The interior view seems not intended to show a boat at all, but to convey the illusion of a drawing room.

It's an approach that seems very foreign to modern boat owners. To our minds, part of the appeal of boating is to feel the sun and wind, to enjoy the tactile relationship with the environment. But our Victorian ancestors had a very different view of the sun, one that they had inherited from still earlier generations. Tanned skin was seen on farm workers, sailors, and others whose occupations required them to spend all day outdoors. Proper ladies and gentlemen could afford

This angle of Heather Belle *has often been photographed over the years, with a variety of different people sitting in the captain's chair. The boat is now infused with the spirit of its current owners, Graeme and Phyllis Ferguson, who have poured a tremendous amount of passion into its restoration. "They have a personal relationship with this boat, and to me, in this painting, it's as if Graeme is still sitting in that chair," said Dunford.*

to be indoors, and when ladies ventured outside they were never so burdened that they did not have a free hand to hold a parasol. In such a culture, it made perfect sense to build boats that offered complete protection from the sun, boats in which the passengers could ride in a comfortably-equipped drawing room.

The hard tops and glass windows had another practical use, since they also kept out the rain. A 36-foot displacement hull boat like *Heather Belle* has a maximum speed of around eight knots; the 28-foot *Our Cup of Tea* is even slower. In boats like this, there is no such thing as running ahead of a fast-rising storm, and even modern owners of these boats have occasion to appreciate the roof.

Practical considerations may have dictated that these cruisers should have a fixed top and windows, but aesthetics influenced their design. *Heather Belle* is a masterpiece of elaborate woodwork, her carved mahogany interior crafted by skilled hands. The ceiling is arched, supported by a series of parallel arches that would have looked striking even if left unadorned. But the builders who crafted this vessel preferred adornment, and so each arch is capped with a piece of carved trim. It's a detail that's easy to overlook at first glance, but it gives the vessel a luxurious feel, and a sense of completion.

Similar details abound throughout the boat. At the end of each bench, a column reaches from the floor to the ceiling, topped with an elaborately carved capital that would seem more at place in a church than in a boat. The rails connecting the columns to the cabin wall are shaped and carved, and the spindles that fit into them are each custom-fitted.

Our Cup of Tea is not quite as elaborate, reflecting both a different era and perhaps a more utilitarian purpose in its original commission. But it too has been put together with a keen aesthetic sensibility, and its beauty has been enhanced by the craftsmen commissioned to restore and rebuild it.

Historically and geographically, these boats seem to have more differences than similarities. They were built in different countries and eras, with different power plants and for different purposes. Queen Victoria was in her last year of life when *Heather Belle* was created. Steam was on its way out, but gasoline engines were still experimental and unreliable and so the boat was originally equipped with an alco-vapor engine. Thirty years later, when *Our Cup of Tea* came along, gasoline was a reliable fuel and alco-vapor engines were no more than quaint antiques. By 1931, production line methods had been successfully brought to the world of boat building, and there was little demand for carved wooden columns, plush drapes, or hand-turned spindles.

But at their heart, these boats are part of the same family. They share a way of relating to the water, a gentility that was seen even earlier in the steam yachts and sailing yachts of the 19th century. Some boats can perform well even if they don't look good; these are boats which have to be beautiful in order to fulfill their real purpose. They are not only stylish, they are boats which make their passengers feel graceful.

Hugh Nevin was disappointed when the red and white maple leaf flag was chosen as Canada's national emblem. He felt the best flag for the country was blue and white with three red maple leaves growing from a single stem. As one of the owners of the Adgie, Nevin flies his preferred flag on the stern whenever he's at the wheel. The remaining flags on the boat change depending on who's on board. She's been seen with a Welsh dragon at the bow in honour of the Nevin family heritage, a German pennant when German guests are aboard, or — as seen in this painting — an American port flag.

10   At Home on Tondern Island

Some boats are famous for their travels, bought and sold and moving from lake to lake — even continent to continent — with each transaction. Some are renowned because they never leave the waters where they were built. Then there are others, like the *Adgie*, that travel only once, from the builder to the buyer, and never again depart.

The *Adgie* was built in Kingston, Ontario, but her real home is the waters of Babies Bay on Lake Muskoka. Aside from the accident of her launching yard, the entire century of this boat's history has been lived within five miles of Babies Bay on Tondern Island.

C.O. Scull, a trust company president from Maryland, commissioned the boat in 1907, hiring the Davis Dry Dock Company of Kingston to build her. Forty-eight feet long and 11.29 tons, she was powered by steam, propelled sedately through the water by a boiler that produced a nominal 4.8 horsepower.

Although varnished wood would later become popular, painted white hulls were the style of the day, and *Adgie* was nothing if not stylish. Tondern Island was the most fashionable part of Lake Muskoka, site of the elegant and lovely cottages that would become known as Millionaires Row at a time when millionaires were as rare as billionaires are today. It was an area where servants were employed to maintain the grand homes and the elegant boats, and the *Adgie* looked entirely at home there. Her hull glistened, its fresh white paint on a July afternoon almost too bright to look at. The brass gleamed with pride and polish and bright flags fluttered from her bow and stern as she cruised the waters around Beaumaris.

While the hull was white, the superstructure was varnished oak and mahogany. The long, elegant cabin was fitted with deep leather benches on both sides and interior cabinetry in dark and blonde mahogany. There was a galley and a head, of course, and a suitably nautical perch at the bow for the captain, his high wooden seat fastened to the deck on a pair of sliding brass tracks.

She lived at the end of Babies Bay, a shallow and rocky bay on the north end of the island where the Scull family and several of their friends and relatives had cottages. A long green boathouse was constructed for her, for it takes a special building to house 48 feet of boat. That boathouse would remain her home for 60 years, even as the ownership of the boat changed.

C.O. Scull named the boat for his wife Ann, who was known to her friends as Adgie. When Mr. Scull died, he left the boat to his wife's nephew, Wilson Book, and the boat soon became known to many in the area as The Book Boat. The Books used the boat regularly, not only for the social cruises and picnics for which she was designed, but even for fishing trips, casting lines from the spacious stern deck or trolling the waters at a sedate pace.

A steam yacht is elegant and charming, but it is not without its drawbacks. It requires the services of a licensed engineer, the boiler and engine occupy an enormous amount of space amidships, and spur-of-the-moment departures need to be delayed while the boat gets up a head of steam. These inconveniences were acceptable when the *Adgie* was built, for the main alternative was one of the new and notoriously unreliable internal combustion engines. But by the 1930s, gas and diesel motors had been refined and steam was an anachronism, so a diesel engine was installed. The new power plant was an improvement, but it would have been wrong to remove the elegant smokestack that gives the vessel its distinct look. And so it remained in place, a delicious salute to a bygone era, whose ersatz nature is revealed to all who peer in the windows and see that the stack connects to absolutely nothing.

The *Adgie* wasn't the only steam yacht of her type on the lake. Every family of note, it seemed, had its own steam yacht or a smaller steam launch, and early photographs show them lining the docks at regattas or waiting alongside the larger steamships to pick up guests arriving by train in Gravenhurst or Bala. In fact, the *Adgie* had a sister ship, the *Phoebe II*, which lived a couple of kilometres from Babies Bay on Urania Island.

The *Adgie* changed hands several times over the years, going from the Sculls to the Books to the Bergers. But while the ownership moved around, the boat didn't. All of the owners lived around Babies Bay and none of them felt it necessary to move the boat, so the green-shingled boathouse remained her home.

But time is not always kind to old boats, and by the 1960s, the *Adgie* was obviously past her prime. It was time for her to leave the old boathouse, and she was given to Francis Fowler, the boatman who had most recently been charged with keeping her running.

Fowler took the boat to his home, a waterfront property near the bridge that connects Tondern Island to the mainland, a mere four kilometres by water, or a kilometre by land from Babies Bay. He had dreams of restoring the *Adgie* to her former glory, but it wasn't to be and for nearly 20 years the boat sat there, neglected and quietly decaying.

In 1986, though, a new group of enthusiasts came along. Four families from the area pooled their resources to buy the boat and have her restored. It didn't take much money to buy the old girl — the purchase price was a mere $6,000 — but the restoration would cost many times that. Rotten planks were replaced, and the superstructure was rebuilt in mahogany, reinforced with enough strength that guests would be able to sit atop the roof and enjoy the view. Since the historical accuracy of the boat had been compromised by removing the steam engine many decades earlier, the owners had no hesitation adding other modern conveniences such as a sound system and a microwave oven in the galley. But the look and feel of the boat, from the art deco fold-down sink in the head to the throaty roar of the steam whistle, remain intact.

Once renovations were underway, the four families considered the old question of where to house such a boat. One of the group, Bill Grand, had enough land on Grandview Island to have a suitable boathouse built which he leased to the other owners. Grandview is just a kilometre south of Tondern, so once again the *Adgie* had a new home in the old neighbourhood.

The *Adgie* doesn't leave the boathouse as often as she once did, certainly not as frequently as in the days when Mr. Book went fishing from the stern every day, but she remains a popular sight whenever she takes a cruise around the waters off Tondern Island. The white paint still gleams, the brass still glistens, and the flags still flutter in the breeze as the elegant vessel makes her way around the waters she knows so well.

11 The Fast and Graceful Vikings

Some boats are celebrated for what's above the water, their graceful lines and sweeping appearance, their well-chosen fittings or remarkable woodwork. Others are notable for what's beneath the hood or below the waterline, an engine that was innovative in its day, a hull design that helps the boat travel at speed or cut sharp turns that leave race competitors bouncing in its wake. Then there are the Ditchburn Vikings, vessels which manage to combine elegant appearance and raceboat-like performance in a way that has rarely been seen.

Introduced in 1928, the Viking design was a popular one with Ditchburn clients, and around 15 were built. Above the waterline, the Vikings are solid contributors to the Ditchburn reputation for building superb-looking boats. The lines are more powerful and muscular than the classic displacement launches of the 1920s, a bit beamier at the bow, but they still retain a feel of elegance. The raised engine hatch leads into a wood-framed windshield similar to those seen on the displacement launches, but where the earlier windshields were mounted at a ninety degree angle to the deck, the Viking windshield slopes toward the driver, a detail that makes the book look fast even before it leaves the dock. The finishing details are impeccable, from the rich leather upholstery to the walnut dash.

With so much beauty above the water it's easy to overlook the feature that makes the Viking unique, but it's an essential part of the popular design. It's only just visible, a break in the smooth waterline about a third of the way back from the bow, a downward cut that marks a break in the hull line. This is the step, and it makes the Viking a remarkable vessel to ride in.

Stepped hulls had been around for a few years when Ditchburn launched the Viking line. Raceboat drivers had discovered years earlier that reducing the amount of boat touching the water was a good way to make a boat go faster. With a step or two in a flat, planing hull, the boat would rise up as it accelerated until only the step and the stern were touching the water. Putting a stepped hull on a raceboat was one thing, though; putting it on a luxurious family boat was another. The result was a unique combination, an elegant launch that could carry the ladies to tea at the yacht club, then peel away from the dock in a blistering display of speed.

It was a combination that appealed to Fred Burgess. In 1928, he entered the Ditchburn showroom in Toronto's Burk's building, and began discussing his options with Tom Greavette, the head of sales for Ditchburn. Greavette showed him a prototype they'd built, and explained that they were launching a new model, the Viking. Burgess was impressed, and in September that year he placed the order.

No details were left to chance in this arrangement — the specifications go on for more than three pages, listing every detail right down to the size of screws that would be used. The purchase price was $5,700, an enormous sum of money at a time when the average working man's salary in Canada was $23 a week.

The boat was named *Mowitza II*, a name suggested by Fred Burgess's sister. She had read a book about a Native man who had a

A Ditchburn Viking like Mowitza II could be depicted at the dock or cruising sedately, but they really look at their best when travelling at speed and riding up on the incredibly effective stepped hull. This painting celebrates how well such a graceful boat can move through the water.

pet deer named Mowitza, which was renowned for its speed. The fleet-footed *Mowitza II* was delivered in June 1929, just in time for the Muskoka Lakes Association regatta. The motorboat races were serious affairs in those days, and the rivalry was intense, but much to the dismay of both Burgess and Ditchburn, *Mowitza II* came second in its class.

Burgess had other cause for complaint as well. The specifications had indicated the deck would be bookmatched, with planks on either side cut from the same piece of wood so the grain and colour matched exactly. He didn't feel the work was up to Ditchburn's usual standard. Furthermore, he had seen *Mint Julep*, another Viking built for Lady Eaton, and had noted that it had features his did not — a silver instrument panel mounted on a walnut dash plate, and two tiny shelves located at either end of the dash. Ditchburn responded to his complaints immediately, promising to redo the deck and the dash over the winter.

In 1930, with the aesthetics taken care of, it was time to address that nagging matter of a second place finish. Early on race day, Burgess brought the boat to the Ditchburn plant in Gravenhurst. It was lifted out of the water and dried for a few hours, then the hull was burnished with graphite to reduce friction. Back in the water it was fueled with a mere 15 gallons of fuel — enough to get to the regatta and run the race. To give it a bit of extra oomph, ten ounces of ether was added to the tank. Burgess paid $16 for the work.

At the race, *Mowitza II*'s main rival was Ewart McLaughlin's *Whippet*. It should have been no contest — *Whippet* was an out-and-out raceboat, capable of trouncing even a fast launch like *Mowitza II*.

But McLaughlin, the son of General Motors founder Sam McLaughlin and a veteran boat racer, was also a sportsman who believed in giving the fans something to watch. For the first half of the race he held back, allowing *Mowitza II* to stay close by. In the final lap he put the throttle forward to claim the victory, only to see a spray of oil from a burst oil line. *Mowitza II* crossed the line first, claiming the open race trophy.

Burgess raced the boat again and again, winning the class at least three more times. Pre-race preparations in later years became even more elaborate, and included removing the windshield and installing a canvas cover on the forward cockpit to reduce wind drag.

The boat was treasured for several years, but time is not always kind to old raceboats, for there's always something faster coming along. In 1935, that something was *Curlew*. It was a radical new design from the Greavette boatworks, a cigar-shaped boat called a Streamliner, and *Curlew* soon found a preferred place in Fred Burgess's boathouse. Beside it, the once-innovative *Mowitza* began to look old and tired, and it wasn't long before the old girl was being towed down the lake.

But even though it could no longer win races, a Ditchburn Viking was still an impressive boat. *Mowitza II* changed hands a few times, and has been restored and repowered more than once. And even as it nears 80 years of age, the hull design continues to impress, She will travel comfortably at 50 miles per hour, rising straight up out of the water and getting up "on step" the way she always did. *Mowitza II* is still a fleet-footed deer.

There are some angles which seem natural when painting or photographing a particular boat. A 35-foot launch like Marco is often shown from above, in order to capture the extremely long foredeck. What's often overlooked, though, is the lovely long sheerline found on such a boat. To see that you need to look at the boat from water level. Dunford has painted this boat several times, and almost always includes the family dog, who frequently rides in this family boat.

12 Minett–Shields: A Partnership Like No Other

The world of boat building has always been a realm of strange partnerships, a place where solitary artisans who can craft exquisite boats meet as equals with the wealthy boat-lovers who can pay for their services. They aren't supplier and customer, buyer and seller, they are partners in a symbiotic relationship in which each recognizes and appreciates that the other has something they need, be it skill or money. Neither can achieve their goals without the other.

The partnership between buyer and builder may be odd, but surely the most unusual partnership in the world of wooden boating was the strange coming together of a salesman and a builder. It would be difficult to find two more different individuals than Bryson Shields and Bert Minett — one a poised and graceful gentleman, the well-bred son of a wealthy family; the other a socially awkward, perpetually rumpled son of the backwoods. But they shared a love of life in Muskoka, and an absolute passion for boats, and together they produced some of the finest boats Muskoka has seen.

Bryson Shields was born on May 25, 1900. Five weeks later, on July 1, he travelled with his family on their annual holiday to the family's summer home at Foot's Bay, a fact which was duly noted in a handwritten entry on the wall of the family's cottage. The family was typical of many early Muskoka cottagers. Patrician and well-cared-for at home in Brampton where Shields's grandfather had built a successful manufacturing business and been elected the city's first mayor, they came to Muskoka each summer to appreciate a more simple way of life, swimming, eating in the open air, and, of course, boating.

The Shields family launch was the *Idyloak*, named for their cottage. Its builder was Bert Minett, and one of the boat's early adventures perhaps best captures the difference between the two men. In 1914, Britain and her Empire declared war on Germany. When war was declared, Canada's Prime Minister was on holiday at the Royal Muskoka on Lake Rosseau, one of the finest hotels in the Empire. He needed to quickly return to Ottawa, which meant travelling by water to the train station at Foot's Bay, but the hotel didn't have an appropriate launch available. Somebody quickly got word to the Shields family, knowing they had a boat that was available and was sufficiently elegant to carry the Prime Minister. Bryson's father did not care to drive the *Idyloak* so he sent his 14-year-old son to do the job. The Prime Minister caught his train at Foot's Bay, unaware that he was conveyed there in the first collaborative venture between the personality of Shields and the craftsmanship of Minett.

Shields grew into the sort of man other men envy and women love — poised, wealthy, charming and handsome. A superb dancer and an elegant dresser ("some people put on clothes," said his wife, Eva, "but Bry really *wore* them"), he moved easily in the wealthy circles which family money opened to him. Educated at Trinity College, a private school in Port Hope, then at the University of Toronto, he soon moved to New York City where his uncle had a successful textiles firm. With no children of his own the uncle hoped to train Bryson to take over the business, but Shields found textiles to be boring, and decided to pursue something else. He left his uncle's employ in a suitably dramatic fashion: an uncle on his mother's side, an executive with Standard Oil, was passing through New York en route from Ceylon to Holland, and hosted a party on board ship prior to sailing. Shields attended the party, and either didn't hear or chose to ignore the call for departure. The ship pulled away with Shields aboard; he sailed to Holland with a dinner jacket as his only luggage, then landed a job with Quaker Oats and stayed in Europe for four years.

Eventually, though, he made his way back to Canada, and to Muskoka, where the craftsman Bert Minett was struggling to keep his business afloat.

Shields was ten years old when the first Minett boatworks opened on the Muskoka River, and he was just 25 when he returned to Canada and found a firm in trouble. Minett had lost a key staff member when designer Bert Hawker left to serve overseas in 1914, returning after the war to take up employment at the Ditchburn boatworks. But that problem could be overcome since designers like his old employer John Hacker were available for hire, selling stock hull designs or designing new hulls to meet the customer's specifications. Minett could use the works of other designers below the waterline, and draw on his own inimitable artistic talents to create something extraordinary above the waterline. The larger problem had to do with Minett's craftsmanship. Bert Minett was arguably the finest craftsman of his age, a superb woodworker and an artistic genius with a solid understanding of naval engineering. There was no aspect of boat building that he did not do well. No aspect, that is, other than the business side. Minett was not a born salesman. His focus was on boats, not people, and he was often ill-at-ease in the company of strangers. He wasn't one to talk somebody into buying his boats.

That was not the major challenge facing his business, since Minett's boats were so good the customers continued to come through the door. Minett simply believed in the perfectibility of every boat, and would strive for that perfection at any cost. If a boat didn't look exactly right when it was done, he would take it apart and do it again until it was right. It didn't matter that the customer was waiting, or that the cost of paying his men to redo the work would eliminate any profit on the boat. It simply had to be done.

The results were predictable. By 1925, even though orders were still coming in the door, the company was nearly bankrupt, its employees owed six months of back wages. It didn't just need a manager, it needed a saviour. It needed Bryson Shields.

Shields bought into the company, which was renamed Minett-Shields in September 1925. He took control of the finances and the sales, but had enough sense to leave boat building entirely in Minett's hands. The boats the new firm produced were still just as fine as ever — in fact, Minett continued to win over customers and lose money by rebuilding boats when he felt it was necessary, but under Shields's direction this was no longer a serious problem.

Before Shields came aboard Minett had been doing a booming trade in 26-foot displacement hull launches, and demand for them continued for several years. *Onnalinda*, which was launched less than a year after Shields entered the business, is fairly typical of these boats. Built for a Dr. Graham of Montreal, it was named after the point on Lake Joseph where Dr. Graham had his cottage. Like many boats of its era, the boat has little in the way of adornment. There is minimal deck hardware and little additional flair, but the quality of Minett's workmanship ensures that the stripped-down style looks clean rather than minimalist, that the lack of adornment showcases the purity of the boat's form. It's a boat that looks well-proportioned and finely finished, as well as riding well and handling nicely. Little

Bert Minett understood that clean, uncluttered lines can make a powerful statement, and his 1920s launches like Onnalinda *demonstrated that awareness. The perfectly symmetrical point of view captures and enhances the boat's unadorned beauty.*

It features a beautiful Minett-Shields launch, but this painting is really about water and light. Eaglet II becomes simply a beautiful adjunct to this ethereal scene, a lovely addition that complements and enhances the play of sunlight on the waves.

wonder, then, that it has remained a treasured part of Muskoka. *Onnalinda* stayed at the cottage on Lake Joseph even after the Graham family sold the cottage. It was fully restored in the 1990s and brought to gleaming perfection by Butson Boats. In fact, the restoration was so good that the owner was afraid of scratching it, which took the pleasure out of driving it. The *Onnalinda* was sold, and now resides in another old Muskoka boathouse near Beaumaris where it enjoys regular — but respected — use.

The most impressive boats to come out of the Minett-Shields shop were the big showpieces, enormous launches with an equally large presence on the water. *Eaglet II* is among these dramatic beauties. At 36 feet, it is one of the largest launches built by Minett-Shields, and every inch of it speaks of quality workmanship. As with *Onnalinda* the deck hardware is minimal, but there are fine details to be found throughout the interior. The dash is ornate, the split windshields located fore and aft (one for the driver, one for the passengers at the rear of the main cockpit) cleverly designed to swivel open or closed. The coaming around the front cockpit is decorated with carved scrollwork, a simple and elegant detail but one which required many hours of labour by Bert Minett or one of his skilled employees. The deck planking is particularly noteworthy, showing the attention Minett lavished on every aspect of his boats. Some builders would have been satisfied with simply using wood of superior quality, but that wasn't sufficient for Minett. Even after the wood had been carefully selected for grade, he would study the grain in the individual planks to ensure each plank complemented the ones on either side of it. It goes without saying that the planks would be bookmatched, so that the pattern of grain on one side of the deck was repeated on the other.

Like all of Minett's boats, of course, it handles beautifully. The hull is a modified displacement shape, smooth and round toward the bow, but transitioning to a hard chine at the stern. The result is a smooth ride at low speeds, and a dry, stable planing surface at speed.

This same hull shape was used five years later, when Robert John McKay ordered the *Marco*. The first two years of the Depression had been difficult years for Minett-Shields, as they were for boat builders everywhere. But by 1932 a few orders were trickling in again. McKay and his wife, Eva Marco McKay, owned Marco Island near Beaumaris, and their decision to purchase a grand new launch was welcome news at Minett-Shields. The business had been operating off-and-on for a couple of years, and a contract to build a 34-foot launch meant a bit more work for the boat builders. Bert Minett had always worked alongside his employees, and that was particularly true in the early 1930s when work was scarce. Years later he told *Marco's* third owner that he had built the boat himself, and there seems no reason to doubt it. Like *Eaglet II* and the other big launches the company produced, *Marco* is a picture of elegance.

The boat has left Marco Island, and now resides at Sappho Island. It's still used regularly for evening cruises — "Marco cruises" as the owners call them — although it's not used to run errands as often as it once was. When boats are jostling for a spot at a crowded dock on Lake Muskoka, notes current owner Margie McCallum, "nobody wants to see you arrive in a 34-foot boat!"

Marco was one of the last big launches Bert Minett built as an owner of the company. In 1934 he gave up his stake in the business that bore his name. He kept working at Minett-Shields for several more years, though, before moving to Hamilton to build boats for the war effort. Minett-Shields closed its doors in 1952, not long before Bert Minett returned to Bracebridge from Hamilton. Both Bert Minett and Bryson Shields remained in Bracebridge until their deaths — Minett passed away in 1966, Shields died in 1975. The factory on Bracebridge Bay where their unique partnership had thrived was torn down in the 1980s, the land converted into a park.

The sweep of light is an important element in this painting, creating a dramatic contrast between light and dark.
The boat has no name, and never has had one as far as its current owner knows.

13   Boat Building Outside Muskoka

The history of boat building in Muskoka is a story of historical accidents, a confluence of characteristics that made the rise of the boat building trade all but inevitable. The region has water — thousands of kilometres of shoreline, hundreds of islands, lakes and rivers. It had settlers who needed boats and wealthy visitors who wanted them.

The region is not completely unique. There are other regions in North America where that same confluence occurred, where wealthy visitors built homes along extensive waterways, creating a demand for boats and a clientele who could afford to pay for them. Boats were built there, too, and while few of them reached the heights of craftsmanship and artistry displayed by the Muskoka builders, they remain treasures in their own right.

One of those regions is found in eastern Ontario, where the inland sea that is Lake Ontario gives way to the mighty river. Sail past the city of Kingston, and round the enormous bulk of Howe Island, a chunk of land so large that it constitutes a township all on its own, and you've arrived in the Thousand Islands. On and on they stretch, more than 1,800 islands scattered along 80 kilometres of waterway. A menace to sailors in the 18th century, the Thousand Islands became a vacation haven in the late 19th century, a summer refuge for the wealthy who travelled up from the great industrial cities of the northeastern U.S. and built palatial homes on both sides of the international boundary.

It is little wonder that boat builders found a demand for their skills amid the cottages of the Thousand Islands. Eventually there were dozens of builders working on both sides of the border, as many if not more than were working in Muskoka. Others plied their trade farther inland. In Canada they set up shop north of the river along the Rideau system, an aquatic highway that connects Ottawa to Kingston via a series of lakes, rivers and canals. In the U.S. there was another group of builders working south of the St. Lawrence in the vacation lakeland of upstate New York.

In early days these builders might have existed as isolated clusters, with designers on the Rideau Lakes rarely seeing or having a chance to learn from the experiments taking place a few hundred kilometres to the south in the Finger Lakes. Boats from the two regions would have developed in very different ways. But by the beginning of the 20th century, the world had shrunk considerably. The boat builders may have rarely left their own towns and villages but their clients certainly travelled, and if a builder on Lake George or the Rideau River came up with a technique that made his boats go faster, stay drier, or just look better, it wasn't long before his competitors from miles away were hearing about it.

That trend increased as boat builders began travelling. The chief builder at the Jeffreys boatworks on the Rideau River had worked for both Chris-Craft and Dodge before coming to eastern Ontario, and he brought some of their ideas with him. Marine architect

Douglas Van Patten may be best known for his work at Greavette, but there are a number of boats built by Dowsett on the shores of Big Rideau Lake that were either designed by Van Patten or were based on his designs.

"In those days everybody took a page from each other's books," said Jimmy Potter, a boat restorer and an authority on the boats of eastern Ontario. "They looked at what the others were doing, took what worked and left what didn't."

The Gilbert Boatworks in Brockville certainly wasn't immune from that tendency. Established in 1904, it produced skiffs and sculls and sailing canoes, and it soon earned a reputation for its motor launches. The boats were well built and finely appointed, with elegant hardware and pleasant lines, and they sold well and travelled widely. The company had a few construction methods that made the boats unique — most notably it is one of the only firms to use thin strips of light Sitka spruce wood instead of deck compound in the seams of its decks, a much more labour-intensive approach but one which produced an extremely stable and watertight deck — but ask any boat authority to describe Gilbert boats and the same phrase comes up again and again: "they look a lot like a Ditchburn." In fact, even an expert like Potter acknowledges that it can be a challenge to tell the two boat builders apart.

There's no indication of any direct link between Gilbert and

Ditchburn. It seems much more likely that the smaller builder was simply copying the apparent style of the boats that were being produced by the largest builder in the country. Their designs and look were selling well in Muskoka, so they should probably sell in the Thousand Islands as well.

To some extent they did — Gilbert was a prolific builder by eastern Ontario standards, producing a number of well-received boats. But, like all the Canadian builders in eastern Ontario, the company was unable to reach the same heights scaled by Ditchburn or, in later years, Greavette. There was simply too much competition from the U.S. side of the river.

Boat builders may have copied each other extensively, but by the 1920s American boats had developed a very different look and feel. The typical Canadian launch of the era has a displacement hull with the cockpit located behind the engine. The lines are fine and elegant, genteel even. It's a similar look to the Thames River launches that were being built in England. Canadian builders saw these English boats when they were serving overseas during the First World War, and recognized that they sprang from the same inspiration as their own boats, which had in turn been influenced by the boats their British-born grandfathers had built.

American builders, though, had gone in a very different direction. In the 1920s they abandoned the rear cockpit in favour of a forward cockpit. Displacement hulls had been replaced by planing hulls, and the lines had become much thicker, more brawny. Even if one doesn't know the name of the builder, it's nearly impossible to confuse a 1920s American boat with a Canadian boat of the same era. Muskoka builders could afford to ignore these trends for a few years. Many people preferred to buy a boat that was built nearby. On Muskoka's lakes there weren't many independent marinas, so servicing was largely done by the builders. And the quality of the Muskoka-built boats was so high, with several world-class builders competing to outdo each other in design, construction and finish, that there was no incentive for a boat-buyer to go looking for an assembly line boat from another area.

In the Thousand Islands, though, builders had a lot more competition in the neighbourhood. A cottager in the Thousand Islands could buy a Canadian-style launch from Gilbert or Dowsett, or he could buy an American-style launch from any number of builders on that side of the border. Hutchinson Boatworks and Fitzgerald and Lee were in the neighbourhood, Fay and Bowen and several others were not far away. Even the big builders were not that distant by rail, so small shops like Gilbert found themselves competing with the likes of Gar Wood, Dart, Sea Lyon, Chris-Craft and Hacker.

Ditchburn and Minett-Shields finished their boats to a superlative degree, giving them the subtle and superior custom touches that elevated them from good boats to works of art, and making them stand out when compared to the larger American marques. But while Gilbert didn't reach the heights scaled by Ditchburn, Gilbert boats remain popular with wooden boat lovers. It was the early 1990s when Murray Hogarth came across a 26-foot Gilbert that had been built in 1928. Its history has been lost, and if it ever had a name, that too has been forgotten. The boat was in pieces when Hogarth first saw it, a restoration project that had been abandoned when the former owner ran out of funds. But Hogarth recognized the boat as exactly the sort of vessel he'd been looking for. "I was looking for a Ditchburn or that type of boat, but it didn't necessarily have to be a Ditchburn," he said.

"I recognize that a Ditchburn or a Minett would be much more valuable on the Muskoka lakes. But I'm from eastern Ontario originally, so I thought the Brockville boat was quite attractive."

Hogarth purchased the boat and had the restoration work completed. It now occupies a place in his Muskoka boathouse, and is used frequently. "It's the kind of boat you take out if you want to go for an evening cruise, but on the other hand it will travel distances at 18 or 19 miles an hour. It moves along," Hogarth said. "If it's at all rough, it will cut the wave as all those displacement hulls do."

Nearly 80 years ago, some unknown buyer chose to purchase a new boat from the Gilbert boatworks. It's quite likely that he was motivated by exactly the same factors that inspired Murray Hogarth to purchase the same Gilbert several generations later. The boat was the size he needed, the style he wanted. It was an attractive boat, a usable boat, a Canadian boat.

*Dunford confesses he's at a loss when asked why he so often paints boats from an aerial perspective. There is freedom,
a weightlessness to be had when looking down in a bird's-eye view. "The main reason, I suppose, is that I just love that perspective."
Gem is one of the earliest surviving Greavettes, a boat built when the company was pinning its hopes on production-line boat building.*

14 A New Player Enters the Game

In 1929, Tom Greavette made a momentous decision. A key figure at Ditchburn boats, the man in charge of sales and a director of the company since its incorporation in 1907, he decided the time had come to go out on his own.

Herb Ditchburn's approach to building and selling boats was to focus on the custom market. Greavette felt that had been all very well during the early years of the century, but production lines were the wave of the future. Ford's automobiles had paved the way a couple of decades earlier, and production lines were gradually making their way into other industries. Chris Smith of Chris-Craft had brought the technique to the boat building world, and by the mid-1920s his company was producing three boats a day at a lower cost than many of his competitors. Gar Wood, Horace Dodge and other builders soon followed suit.

Rather than employ a team of skilled boat builders, each of whom had the talent and knowledge to take a single boat through to completion, the new method divided the work into separate tasks. One group of men built hatches, another built frames, another installed planks, and so on. At the end of the line was a crew that could bring all the different components together. Not only was production speeded up, but labour costs were lower for the unskilled and semi-skilled men who could now do much of the work.

In the 1920s, when the economy was booming and customers were plentiful, this approach brought financial success. Soon all the big American builders were expanding. In 1929, Gar Wood moved to a modern plant in Michigan; that same year Horace Dodge, whose company was already building five boats a day, built the largest boatworks in the world, a 210,000-square-foot factory in Newport News, Virginia where workers could build dozens of hulls at once. Greavette, backed by a number of Ditchburn's wealthy clients, decided to move in the same direction.

The new firm was originally called Rainbow Boats, an attempt to capitalize on the fame of Harry Greening's series of Ditchburn-built raceboats, all named *Rainbow*. Herb Ditchburn objected strenuously, and so the new company was named for Tom Greavette. Rather than design new boats from scratch, Greavette made arrangements with Dart Boats of Toledo, Ohio, a successful builder of runabouts that had launched a national advertising campaign in 1929 that was making the Dart name well known. Greavette purchased the licence, designs and hardware to build four of the Dart models — two 18-footers (the Ensign and the Roamer), the 23-foot Mohawk, and the 26-foot Comet.

Hopes ran high in late 1930 as construction crews began work on the new Greavette boatworks. When it opened in the spring of 1931 it employed more than 40 men working on both day and night shifts, and its backers were confidently predicting that demand would soon force them to expand the plant and the payroll. But in boat building, as in life, timing is essential, and Greavette's timing could not have been worse. What had started as a shock to the financial markets in October 1929 had quickly deepened into a full-blown depression. In tough financial times, it was easy to put off buying a new boat and make do with the old one instead, and every boat builder in the country was forced to slow down production. The plant operated at full speed for a couple of months, but with few sales it was soon closing periodically, only opening again when there were enough orders to warrant it. In 1933 Greavette reorganized the company, abandoned the production model approach, and returned to custom boat building.

The workers at Greavette built 31 Dart boats. Sales may have been slow — in fact, the company was still offering them in 1933, a year after the Dart boat company itself had gone out of business — but the boats themselves were quite good. Although they were built in a production-line fashion, and were produced as stock models with few options available, they were well-designed, lovely craft. The foredeck in particular shows subtle and pleasing lines, with a compound curve that runs side to side and fore and aft before sweeping up slightly at the windshield. All of the Dart models featured a forward drive configuration, with the driver positioned in front of the engine rather than to the rear. In the triple cockpit models like the Mohawk, the third cockpit was positioned behind the engine, while the double cockpit models were built with both cockpits forward of the engine. American builders had adopted the forward position as the standard some years earlier, but it had taken until the late 1920s for it to become accepted in Muskoka.

Dart boats were also designed to appeal to customers who didn't own a boathouse, or even own waterfront property. Most wooden boats need to spend a bit of time in the water prior to their first ride each spring. The wooden planks dry out in the air, but once the boat is back in the water the planks swell up, pressing tight against each other and making the hull watertight. The Dart boats, though, were built with a double hull, with a layer of rubberized canvas between the inner cedar planks and the outer mahogany planks. They were promoted as a boat which could be launched and driven right away.

It may have been the canvas in the hull, it may have been the lines, or possibly it was the price that convinced the Herman family of Toronto's Herman Furs to buy one of the 23-foot Mohawk models. With six children at the cottage on Lake Simcoe, they needed a boat that would carry everyone. The triple cockpit Mohawk seemed to be just the thing. The price was surely right — only the seventh Mohawk built by Greavette, it was a demonstrator model that had been used by Grew Boats, a Lake Simcoe boat builder and marine operator that had been an agent for Greavette. In 1933 the Mohawk made its way to the family cottage, where it would remain for more than 30 years. It was named *Belle II* after Mrs. Herman, whose first name was Belle.

In the late 1960s, *Belle II* was taken out of service and put into storage, first in a boathouse, and then in a field under a tarp. After a few years of neglect, it was purchased by a trio of would-be fixer-uppers, who tinkered with the boat off and on for several more years. Finally, in 1988, it came into the hands of Ted and Sharon Johnson.

"Sharon and I had been looking casually for an old boat for 10 years, without the means to do anything with one if we found it," Ted explained. "But it was fun, an excuse to go around the big Muskoka lakes." Ted came by his love of wooden boats naturally — his great-great-uncle was Albert Sydney Smith, who founded Port Sydney on Mary Lake, and whose many business interests included running a supply boat named *Gem*. Ted's grandfather had often travelled on Uncle Sydney's steamer, and had eventually acquired his own boat, a 1919 Minett on which Ted later learned to drive, and which is still in service on Lake Joseph.

Despite spending several years under a tarp, *Belle II* was still in fair shape. The varnish had lifted, of course, and the compound between the deck seams needed to be replaced. The rubberized canvas was rotten, as were some of the inner hull planks and much of the topsides woodwork. The original Scripps engine was gone, but it had been replaced with a Kermath Sea Queen that is at least appropriate to the period. And the boat had all the original hardware, including the silver-plated instrument cluster, and the decorative arrow that was mounted on the sides in reference to the Dart boat company. The outer bottom was in such good shape that Ted had the restorers at Millar Potter Boatworks reuse the original mahogany planks. Some said it was false

economy, he acknowledges, but he wanted the boat to be as original as possible.

The boat was given a new name prior to being launched on Mary Lake. *Gem*, it's now called, named for the steamer that once famously plied these same waters. The new *Gem* is a staple sight on the lake, carrying six people comfortably and still getting up on plane with ease, just as it did when it was new. It's not the oldest Greavette boat around — Mohawk number three has a home in California — but it's the oldest one still in Muskoka. The two Mohawks and a couple of the 18-foot models are all that remain of the vision that launched Greavette.

Dunford was photographing and studying Gem *one morning, and a flock of ducks swam up and began circling the boat. He knew he had his image. "Painting the ducks in that way makes the boat part of a design, a composition that involves the boat, the water and the ducks, all sharing an environment. Think of all the years that this duck, and her mother, and her mother's mother have adapted and felt comfortable swimming around this boat with us standing on the dock. There's a history to the boat, but there's also a history of this wildlife adapting to mankind and our environment, and feeling comfortable about it."*

The sensuous curves of a post-war Streamliner are absolutely compelling to the eye.
Dunford chose to paint Ad Infinitum from this angle in order to capture the hypnotic curve seen on the right side of the boat.
The effect of the boat's curves is enhanced in this image by the shoreline that is reflected in the gleaming varnish.

Greavette's Greatest Triumphs

"It's like driving a piece of art around the lake. It's just a beautiful piece of sculpture."

In 1933, with his attempt at production line boat building acknowledged to be a failure, Tom Greavette reorganized his company and decided to focus on the thing Muskoka boat builders had always done best, building custom boats. He announced that the new Greavette boats would be designed by John Ludwig Hacker, one of the most renowned boat architects of his day. The combination of Hacker's designs and the boat-building skills of the Muskoka workmen was an immediate success, and the Greavette boatworks was soon producing fast and luxurious launches, and even faster racing runabouts. A wealthy young sportsman named Harold Wilson (whose father was, not coincidentally, the president of the newly reorganized Greavette Boatworks) was soon tearing up the waterways in his Greavette-built *Little Miss Canada* raceboats, which earned the company an enviable reputation among the young gentlemen with a need for speed.

The arrangement with Hacker only lasted a few years, but in that time Greavette produced a boat that was destined to have an enduring effect on Muskoka boat building. It was called *Curlew*, and it launched Greavette's most enduring model, a boat design that would continue to be built for more than 30 years. There are a handful of boat models that even the most unknowledgeable boat fan can name in an instant, and chief among them is the Greavette Streamliner.

What makes the Streamliner's enduring appeal even more remarkable is that it was an extremely stylish design in the 1930s,

and nothing goes out of fashion as quickly as that which is highly stylish. In 1935, the public was completely captivated by the design style that would come to be known as Art Deco (although the term wasn't coined until the 1960s — in the 1930s it was known as Style Moderne, or Modernistic). Art Deco emphasized new and industrial-looking materials, metals and plastics that could be sculpted into round curves that were far removed from the hard edges and sharp lines used by earlier designers. It influenced skyscrapers like the Empire State Building, furniture, railway cars and graphic design. In the maritime world it influenced everything from steel ocean liners to mahogany runabouts.

Hacker had toyed with streamlining shapes before. The Dolphin Custom Sport Speedsters produced by his Hackercraft company in 1929 had a distinctive streamlined look, and he built several other boats which presaged the development of the Streamliner.

The first Streamliner, *Curlew* was an instant hit on the lakes. There was something about that shape that grabbed the eye and the imagination and would not let go. Long, low and incredibly sleek, it inspired thoughts of speeding railway carriages or even rockets. Even tied up at the dock it looked fast enough to race and challenge one of the airplanes it closely resembled. The lines would have caught attention no matter what construction material was used; the fact that the boat was built of wood made it even more difficult to ignore. One simply could not look at the curvature of the sides without won-

One of the most significant Canadian raceboats ever built, Miss Canada III is a perfect blend of form and function, a boat as fast as she is beautiful. The boat that currently resides on the Muskoka Lakes is what artists call an ectype, a copy made by the original designer. It was built using the original plans and offsets of Doug Van Patten, who oversaw the recreation of a vessel he said was the finest he ever designed.

dering how anyone had been able to shape and bend wood that way.

It was difficult, time-consuming and expensive, and by all rights *Curlew* should have been a one-off design that was never to be repeated. But in 1935, when *Curlew* was built, the economy was changing. The Depression was still raging as far as the working poor were concerned, but people with money — those who had not lost it in the stock market crash — were finding signs of recovery. Investments were starting to bear dividends again, wealth was being created, and more and more people were finding they could indeed afford the little luxuries like a $15,000 launch. Streamliners were never produced in large numbers, but every now and then another customer would walk through the doors with a craving for something rounded and sleek.

By the late 1930s the design had proved itself to be a winner, and Tom Greavette knew it would remain in the company catalogue for some time to come. In order to keep it fresh, the design needed to be upgraded, the concept perhaps taken even further. John Hacker was now working for Minett-Shields, so the task of redesigning the Streamliner was given to the company's new chief designer, a young man named Douglas Van Patten.

Van Patten was a remarkable designer, someone who knew how to make a boat go fast, but also understood how to make a boat that looked fabulous. When asked to redesign the Streamliner he made a number of modifications to John Hacker's design, most noticeably shortening the boat by turning the torpedo stern into a transom, and exaggerating the rounded lines until the boats looked positively bulbous. Boat-lovers continue to debate the merits of his changes, some insisting the long, double-ended look of the earlier models looks more complete than the square-stern design, but the debate rages in the same way that hockey fans might argue over whether Team Canada 1972 could defeat Team Canada 2000 — it's a pointless,

unwinnable debate between people who, when it comes right down to it, love the same thing. Those who are gripped by a passion for Streamliners would buy any one of them given the chance.

Peter Sharpe knows that passion well. He's loved Streamliners since he was a child, so in 2002 when the chance came to buy a 1947 model, he leapt at it. The boat is named *Ad Infinitum*, and owning it has turned out to be as much of a pleasure as Sharpe had hoped. "It's like driving a piece of art around the lake," he said. "It's just a beautiful piece of sculpture."

That desire to own a movable piece of art kept the Streamliner in production until 1966, longer than any other design in Greavette's history. But it was just one of the designs that helped solidify the reputation of both Greavette and Van Patten.

Quiet and somewhat unassuming, a dreamer and an artist in a world of doers and builders, Van Patten's method of working wasn't always appreciated. Not long after he joined the Greavette firm, Van Patten was asked to rework *Miss Canada II*, a troublesome Hacker-designed raceboat that had been labeled as "too dangerous to drive." He spent an entire day mulling it over and smoking his pipe without doing any apparent work. Company president Ernie Wilson, whose son Harold drove the raceboats, stormed off in disgust. "Let's go home," he said to his son. "He doesn't know what he's doing."

Wilson was wrong. Van Patten's hull modifications turned *Miss Canada II* into a hundred-mile-an-hour racing contender. Once they saw what he could do, the Wilsons told Van Patten they had another challenge: they wanted him to design the fastest boat in the world. He nodded and said quietly, "I know the design that will work."

On December 26, 1937 he began drawing the boat, one he had been planning long before the Wilsons told him they would build it. Two weeks later, the drawings were complete, and by spring, the Greavette Boatworks was ready to unveil *Miss Canada III*. In his long

career, Van Patten designed thousands of boats, from production line vessels to one-off specialty craft, but years later he insisted that *Miss Canada III* was the best boat he had ever designed. It was a triumph of both form and function, with design elements that made the boat look fast and go faster. The breathtaking fore and aft arc of the deck, for example, made the boat look as though it was reaching forward, like a thoroughbred horse extending its neck as it strives for the finish line. And just as the arc of a horse's neck helps it run faster, so too did the arc of the deck help *Miss Canada III*, acting like an aerofoil and providing 900 pounds of lift to the speeding boat.

When all was running as it should, *Miss Canada III* was unbeatable. In 1939 she won the President's Cup in Washington, the first Canadian boat to win the prestigious trophy. She raced before and after the Second World War, was the Canadian National champion, won the national sweepstakes Silver Cup twice, and set a mile straightaway record for Gold Cup boats with a speed of 119 miles an hour. Unfortunately, things did not always go as they should. Mechanical problems plagued her, and again and again she was forced to withdraw from races because of engine failure. In a profile of the contenders for the 1948 Gold Cup race, Yachting magazine said *Miss Canada III* was "A beautiful, tremendously fast and fine-turning [boat]. Unfortunately her enormous crew of gremlins always takes over and louses up her chances."

"Sometimes I think a detail of a boat can tell you more about it than a painting of the entire boat," Dunford said. In this case, the strikingly ornate bow light on Touchwood, *a Greavette Sheerliner, is such a compelling detail that it needed to become the central element of the painting.*

In 1948, *Miss Canada III* was retired. The next year, Van Patten, the Wilsons, and the Greavette boatworks proved that their magic was unabated when they unveiled her replacement, *Miss Canada IV*, a boat that would go on to set a North American speed record of 138.6 miles per hour, with an unofficial top speed of 173 miles per hour.

In between designing and building superb raceboats, the team at Greavette continued to craft remarkable vessels that anyone of means could own. Just after the Second World War a new Van Patten design emerged, a boat that would become Greavette's second longest-lived model: the Sheerliner.

The Sheerliner's concave hull shape was almost exactly opposite to the Streamliner's convex lines when seen from bow on. The effect of that design is immediately felt on a "high water" day, when the wind cuts across the lake and the curling whitecaps keep some boats in the boathouse. Then the Sheerliners are at their best, cutting through the water and shedding waves with impunity.

But it would be a mistake to dismiss the Sheerliner as merely a practical boat. The Sheerliner is still a Van Patten-designed Greavette. In other words it's a beautiful creation, with lines that lead the eye forward no matter which angle the boat is seen from. That's particularly true of *Touchwood*, a 24-foot model built in 1948. The covering boards trace a complex curve, narrow at the stern, broadening amidships, narrowing again at the deck then widening yet again as they meet each other at the bow. The deck planking — 20 pieces in each half of the deck — forms another graceful curve when seen from above, a design which was regrettably dropped in later models. That same curve was repeated in the decking of *Miss Canada IV*, which was built the same year as *Touchwood*.

The curvature of the Sheerliner's deck is similarly complex, a gentle compound angle that rises and falls from side to side, and from fore to aft — a design that gives the boat elegance and style, and which evokes the curvature of the Streamliner without taking it to the same degree.

Another element that seems to have been inspired by the Streamliner is the bow lighting. As with the Streamliners of the post-war era, the bow light on the Sheerliners is built into the bow just behind the cutwater, set off with gleaming chrome plates built into the hull and the deck.

Touchwood is one of the early models in a design that would last for nearly three decades. One of its unique features is a right-hand steering wheel, a placement Van Patten advocated in order to provide more balance to counteract the rotation of the propeller.

Originally named '*Twill Do*, the boat was purchased by Lambert Love who owned Elgin House, a resort that stood on land now occupied by the Lake Joseph Club. Love knew life on the water and understood the value of a good boat, and he looked after this boat with meticulous care. The current owner, Stan Meek, has childhood memories of Love stopping the boat well out in the lake and installing the rope fenders before approaching the dock — something any modern owner of a wooden boat would do as a matter of course, but not a common practice in the days when wooden boats were often regarded as mere transportation. "He was a man of style, a very dignified man," Meek said. "He prized that boat like anything."

The third owner, Meek continues to prize the boat. It is, he says, not only the most beautiful boat he owns, it is the nicest design Greavette built.

Others disagree. Tom Greavette's daughter, Lorraine McNab, was asked a few years ago if there was any boat she still wished she had. Her reply was immediate: a Streamliner. "That to me was the dream boat," she said. "I wish we still had a couple tucked away."

Dunford knew he had to capture action, speed and movement in his image of Shadow, *a small, fast, lively boat.*
The water in the boat's wake shows clearly where it has been, but driver Richard Blair is focused solely on what's ahead, not what's behind.

16
Going Fast, Looking Good

To build a fast boat you need to understand what's going on below the waterline, how turbulence affects drag and how a complex hull line can impact speed and handling. To sell fast boats, though, you also need to understand what's going on above the waterline and inside the buyer's head. A boat that will win races just needs to *be* fast; a boat that will attract buyers also needs to *look* fast.

That principle has long been understood by Muskoka's boat builders, and nowhere was it better applied than in the design that's known today as the gentleman's racer. Built with a hard chine and a planing hull, typically around 18 feet in length, and sometimes equipped with only enough seating for two, they were fast, nimble, and great fun to drive. They're often referred to as sports cars of the water, and with good reason. They weren't terribly practical for a family, but families were not their target market. They were built to appeal to single people in their teens and 20s, young gentlemen who wanted to look sharp, who wanted to feel the wind in their face and to feel the eyes of their admirers as they cut across the water. They were built to go fast and look sexy.

These speedy little sportsters began to appear in Muskoka in the late 1920s, but they really came into their own in the 1930s. Although they were by no means cheap, they were still less expensive than the large launches, and even during the Depression there were still people who could afford to buy a new gentleman's racer. All the major names built them — Ditchburn, Greavette, Minett-Shields — and the designs changed constantly as naval architects tried to tweak a bit more speed out of them.

When they succeeded in getting some more speed, their success was well known. Professional motorboat racing was enormously popular until it was curtailed by the fuel shortages of the Second World War, and tens of thousands of people would gather on the shore in places like Detroit and Toronto to watch the big races. The crowds were smaller in Muskoka, but they were no less enthusiastic. Every bay and lake in Muskoka had a regatta, it seemed, and nearly all of them featured motorboat races as one of the high points.

The season typically began in late July, and would continue every weekend through to the end of August. Boats came from across Muskoka, and even from Barrie and Orillia to compete in these races. Although the drivers were amateurs, many races offered cash purses, and a good driver in a fast boat could win enough in a season to cover his expenses. The boats raced against others of their class, from the big launches with their 200 horsepower engines all the way down to the little Sea Fleas, flat-bottomed boats about the size of a door propelled by an outboard motor. The 100 horsepower class was perfect for small and light gentleman's racers, and competition was enthusiastic. Naturally, the boats that raced in the regattas were also used for fun cruises, and boats like *Shadow* and *Little Miss Canada II* could often be seen ripping around Muskoka's lakes at more than 35 miles an hour with enthusiastic young gentlemen like Charles Wheaton and Harold Wilson at the wheel.

Minett-Shields built *Shadow* for Charles Wheaton in 1933, and it is a superb example of the form. Lines are clean and smooth, with no unnecessary ornamentation. The deck is long and sleek with a sub-

The name of a boat can help define how it should be painted. Black Beauty is an exciting, speedy boat that demanded to be painted in action. The angle of the boat and the angle of the driver's head give it "a horsiness," Dunford said. "There's a thoroughbred quality to this scene."

tle crown, but with nothing that looks superfluous. The forward cockpit is equipped with a flush-mounted hatch — a functional addition when racing, as it reduces wind drag from the empty cockpit, but also a useful way of preserving the integrity of those long deck lines when the hatch is closed. The brightwork was also designed to enhance the feel of speed. The mahogany engine vents are shaped like elongated teardrops, with art deco-inspired chrome accents which make the vents look as though they've been pulled into shape, stretched out by the speed of the boat.

Even before gentleman's racers came on the scene there was a demand for fast boats, and the designs have changed constantly in response to changes in engine technology. That was particularly true in the first three decades of the last century. Boat builders at that time faced a trade-off between power and weight: a bigger engine can produce more power, but the added weight means it must be mounted in a bigger boat which in turn requires more power to move it. In the early 1930s, a 600-pound engine could produce 90 to 100 horsepower — enough to move an 18-foot boat quite handily, but sluggish when asked to push a boat that was 20 feet long. But every few years, it seemed, somebody was coming out with a new engine that offered more power with less weight. By the end of the decade, a 600-pound engine would produce 150 horsepower or more, and boats could be built in a much greater range of sizes. A new generation of sports boats began to emerge in Muskoka, the racing runabouts.

In 1934-35, Minett-Shields built half a dozen of these "grown up sport boats" to a design by John Hacker. Twenty-one and a half feet long, and a good ten inches wider than the gentleman's racers, they were stable enough to handle the added power that came from a flat-head six cylinder engine kicking out at least 140 horsepower. They featured two cockpits, but the controls were mounted in the forward cockpit, just as had become standard in the racing world.

There are at least five of these racing runabouts still on the water, a testament to both their beauty and their performance. Even when they could no longer win races, these boats were so much fun to drive, and so lovely to look at, that their owners held on to them.

It's not known who originally owned *Black Beauty*, or whether the boat was ever raced. It seems likely that it was meant for races, for the boat is built of cedar rather than mahogany. The choice of wood is another one of those trade-offs faced by boat builders who want to build fast boats that look good. Cedar is lighter, which allows the boat to travel faster, but it doesn't varnish as nicely as mahogany. *Black Beauty* achieved both speed and looks by being finished in black, one of the few Minett-Shields boats finished entirely in that colour. Other boat builders have done the same thing, sometimes achieving a compromise by crafting boats with painted black cedar hulls and varnished mahogany decks.

Roger Werner began to fall in love with *Black Beauty* before he even set foot in it. "The first thing that catches your eye in a boat like this is the integrity of the marine architecture. John Hacker never designed a bad boat, and on this one the proportions are just perfect. It's an extremely attractive boat."

When he took it out on the water, he discovered a boat whose handling matches its looks, a boat that is fast, dry, comes up on plane quickly, and turns well in both directions. "It is the nicest combination of a soft ride at displacement speeds and plenty of performance at racing speeds. It's a really nice boat, a really good performer."

"When I went for a ride in it, I decided right away that I had to buy it."

Forward-drive boats like *Black Beauty* may have been the latest fashion in 1934, but Muskoka had not seen the last of the rear-control gentleman's racers. The 1930s Greavette Flash was a well-known stock version of that configuration, and as late as the mid-1960s,

Greavette was building an 18-foot, rear-drive model called the Fireflash. And in 1939, the company produced a custom-designed 19 1/2-foot gentleman's racer designed by Douglas Van Patten.

When it was powered by a 115 horsepower six cylinder engine, *The Jeffrey* was a fast, responsive boat. Repowered in the 1960s with a V-8 engine that produces over 200 horsepower, it became a rocket that blasts across the waves at 50 miles an hour. Many of the other gentleman's racers have also been repowered with V-8 engines, and many owners have discovered that their 18-foot boats weren't designed to handle that much power. Some become difficult to control, or even display an alarming willingness to roll over. But in boat design, a few inches can make a world of difference. *The Jeffrey* is eighteen inches longer, and correspondingly wider, and it handles the additional power with aplomb.

Like all the best gentleman's racers and racing runabouts, *The Jeffrey* is not just about speed, it's also about style and good looks. The skilled craftsmen at Greavette knew how to put together a superb boat, and understood that the wood on a fast boat needs to be tightly fitted and superbly varnished. Tom Greavette once said that the finish on one of his company's raceboats was so smooth that a fly couldn't land on it without slipping and breaking its neck. Those same standards that helped win international races were also brought to bear on sleek runabouts.

There's also a gracefulness to the design, a completeness that reveals designer Van Patten wasn't just concerned with what was going on below the waterline. Peter Breen, who restored, renamed, and copied *The Jeffrey*, points out that the boat has several unique features, including an unusual crown to its deck. When viewed from bow-on, most gentleman's racers have an even, steady arc from one gunwale to the other. On *The Jeffrey*, most of the curvature is in the outer third on each side. The middle third, where the hatch is located, is nearly flat. It's subtle, something the viewer appreciates without fully understanding what they're seeing, but it makes the boat look absolutely perfect.

Onlookers rarely get a chance to study that line, though, for they rarely see boats like *The Jeffrey* at rest. In photos and paintings, they are almost always shown at speed, skipping across the wave or heeled over in an exciting curve. They may have been built to look good at the dock, but their natural element is out in the lake. Rick McGraw, who currently owns *The Jeffrey*, says driving it is like driving a low-slung English sports car. It's a thrilling ride; it's a beautiful sight.

The lovely bow line of The Jeffrey *is fully revealed when the boat is travelling at top speed.*
Even with a camera it can be challenging to capture a scene like this, because the boat moves with such incredible velocity.

A big, fast boat, Scud II *needed to be painted in motion. By showing it slightly heeled over,*
Dunford was able to depict the interior and the exterior, the long sheerline and the triple cockpit configuration.

17

Forward Thinking

When an architect or designer sets out to create a house, a car, or a boat, they must look at their creation from two perspectives at once, thinking about both utility and style. The world contains far too many examples of buildings and boats that succeed in one area yet fail in the other, office towers that take your breath away with their beauty but keep you waiting for an elevator; boats that handle like a dream but look like a log. The standards for both utility and looks keep changing, of course. A quick boat in 1914 was a slow boat by 1925, and a boat whose lines looked sleek and fast in one era looked outdated a decade later. Very often, changes in technology influence changes in aesthetics: the knife-sharp bows of the displacement hulls gave way to the more gentle entry of a planing hull, the high hatches needed to accommodate the big engines of the pre-war era were eventually replaced with flush decks. And boat drivers were moved from the stern of the boat to the front.

The early motorboats put the driver behind the engine, for a purely practical reason: even the most ardent supporters of gas motors had to agree that the early models were balky and unreliable, needing constant attention. That was particularly true in the early raceboats, many of which were driven by two-man teams consisting of a driver and a mechanic. It was obviously much more practical to place the driver and mechanic behind the engine, so they could make adjustments while still watching where they were going. The rear seat position also came in handy when it came to spotting and dousing engine fires — a not infrequent occurrence in the days when even the best engine tended to throw a bit of oil and fuel when it was running at its top end.

As motorboats became more widely available, it was only natural that the stock models would be designed along similar lines to the raceboats. Cottage owners might not be travelling at 50 miles an hour like Harry Greening or the other famous racers, but they could certainly look like Greening in a sporty runabout with a long wooden deck stretching out over the engine. The design was also influenced by carmakers, who built long, low hoods on their most sporty models.

This approach worked well as long as boats were being built with displacement hulls that cut through the water. But it was not long before naval engineers realized they could get their boats to travel much faster if they could get the hulls up, so that they skipped along the surface of the water rather than travelling through it. The result was the planing hull, followed by the stepped hydroplane which helped reduce the friction of the water even further. It worked beautifully, and speed records were shattered year after year. In 1910, Gar Wood set a world speed record of 30 miles an hour; nine years later, Canadian Casey Baldwin topped 70 miles an hour; in 1931, Gar Wood shattered the 100 mile an hour barrier, one of seven new records set since Baldwin's. By contrast, the 1962 record of 200 miles per hour stood for 38 years.

These rapid increases in speed soon made another problem evident. When a planing hull is rising up it always goes bow first, and even when it has reached planing speeds the bow remains higher

The painter Andrew Wyeth has said that when painting an old building, every layer of paint is a year of sun, weather and life. Dunford applies that same philosophy to boats like Utopia, that have had 70 or more years of life. "You can't just splash on some paint and say you're done," he said. "It's only when you build up the layers that the wood in a painting starts to look like real wood. You've got to get enough years in that finish."

than the stern. The effect is more pronounced in some boats than others, but in all of them it can create a visibility problem.

The solution was obvious: move the driver to the bow, so he is sitting at the highest point in the boat. A forward cockpit design appeared in print as early as 1909, but it wasn't until 1920 that the design became popular. The forward-drive Belle Isle Bearcats — sold by the Belle Isle boat company in Detroit with hulls designed and built by Hacker — were a hit, and it did not take long for other builders to copy the layout. Chris Smith and Sons built their first Chris-Craft boats in 1923 and Horace Dodge launched his company that same year, and both firms featured forward cockpits in their designs. Regional builders followed suit, and from San Diego to Minnesota to New York, the forward-drive runabout was the fashion across the United States.

In this, though, as in much else, Muskoka remained unique. Builders here were certainly aware of trends to the south, but they were not quick to embrace the new design. It may have been natural Canadian conservatism, or a local pride that kept them designing the long deck displacement hull boats that had won Muskoka renown. Whatever the reason, it was 1927 before the first forward-drive boats rolled out of the Minett-Shields boat shop, and it would be another year before Ditchburn and other builders followed. Even then there was no great rush to embrace the forward-drive design, and Muskoka builders continued to produce — and find willing customers for — boats with displacement hulls and with the cockpits behind the engine long after the style had been abandoned by other regions.

By 1930, though, the forward-drive design was at least an option throughout Muskoka. Minett-Shields produced three 32-foot forward-drive runabouts — *Glennavey II*, *Jolly Roger*, and *Scud II*. Not true triple cockpit boats, they feature two rows of seats in the front cockpit, with a second, two-person cockpit at the stern. The boats are virtually identical, and all are still — or are back — on the water.

Scud II was built for David Billings Peck, a native of Chicago who had been summering on Lake of Bays since 1908. In the early 1920s he bought Burnt Island and had a cottage and boathouse built there. Although he was wealthy — his family owned one of Chicago's largest dairies — David Peck liked to keep life simple when he was at the cottage, and his Lake of Bays cottage looks decidedly plain compared to the grand estates his peers were building on Lake Muskoka at the time. But when it came to boats, Peck liked to have the best. It was a trait shared by his sons, Edson and Cameron. Edson owned an 18-foot Minett-Shields racer named *Altair*, which he received for his 18th birthday and kept until his death in 2003; Cameron built up one of the largest boat collections Muskoka has ever seen, a fleet of dozens of launches, raceboats and steamers that was stored in Baysville, Huntsville, and on the family island. *Scud II* — like the displacement launch *Scud I* that preceded it — was a family boat, which is not to say it was sedate. Equipped with a powerful and rare six cylinder Hall-Scott engine, it has tremendous torque, and can rise up on its planing hull and clip across the water at speeds that justify placing the driver in a forward cockpit.

In keeping with the high standards of its builders, it is also a beautiful boat, well-proportioned and graceful, with a barrel-like tumblehome at the stern that sets off the rest of the boat nicely. The brightwork is plentiful, with chrome fittings everywhere which include a pleasant split windshield for the rear cockpit, a thoughtful addition to keep the passengers dry and out of the wind.

Early photos of the boat show it with two separate tops, an auto-top similar to those found on convertibles of the day, and a removable hard top with an access hatch in the roof. The auto-top has since disappeared, and the hard top has spent several decades tucked away in storage.

For many years, that's where the rest of the boat was also kept, in storage in a boat shop near Lake Simcoe, until Tim Chisholm heard about it. "It had holes in the hull, and all the hardware was in boxes," he recalled, but he knew as soon as he saw it that this was a boat worth restoring.

Although Minett-Shields built only three boats like *Scud II*, the forward-cockpit design had arrived in Muskoka to stay. During the early years of the Depression, in fact, Bryson Shields drummed up some work for the company by convincing boat owners to have their old boats modified into modern-looking forward drives (the modifications had mixed success, and some boats would later be changed back to a rear-cockpit configuration in order to restore proper handling). The most successful designs, though, were those boats which were built as conceived, with the driver sitting forward of the engine.

Utopia is one such boat. A true triple cockpit design, the 27-footer was built for Allan Neilson in 1933, and later belonged to Bert Minett's nephew, Bill. The stern lines are similar to those seen on *Scud II*, but the cockpit configuration is different, with the driver and his companion seated in the forward cockpit, and all the other pas-sengers settled into two cockpits located behind the engine. All three cockpits are shielded by windshields, but current owner Gary DeGroote acknowledges that it can be a wet ride in the stern. "It throws a lot of water out the sides. You sit high in the front, and it really throws spray behind." But that, he says, is part of the fun. *Utopia* has elegance in its looks, but it's also a fast and nimble boat, one that gives a thrill to passengers, and has even been used to pull wakeboarders.

The forward cockpit was originally conceived for purely practical reasons, but *Utopia* and *Scud II* are complete boats, triumphs of both practicality and aesthetics. When he's asked about his favourite viewpoint from which to look at the boat, DeGroote pauses to consider. It looks gorgeous when seen from the stern cockpits, he says, with all that varnished mahogany stretching out before you — or above you, if the boat is travelling at speed. But the best view of all, and the best reason to place a cockpit in the bow, comes on a sunny afternoon when the boat is roaring across the lake at speed and the driver looks over his shoulder. "What I really like to see is the faces of the people in the rear cockpits, the big smiles on their faces."

18   Unraveling the Mystery

One Saturday each July, thousands of people file onto the docks at Muskoka Wharf for the Antique and Classic Boat Society's annual boat show. Ten thousand people will shuffle past a hundred or so boats on that day, studying them, dreaming about them, reminiscing about the wooden boats they've owned or ridden in or admired since childhood. Every boat is identified. Some have large wooden plaques temporarily mounted at their berths with the history of the boat and its notable achievements enshrined in mahogany and varnish. Others bear a simple sheet of paper with the basic information: owner's name, boat's name, year of construction, builder. What the sheets don't reveal is that occasionally even that basic information is no more than educated guesswork.

Paul Hammond had worked around wooden boats for years before he decided to buy one. The owner of a successful trucking firm in Bracebridge, he was often called on to move large wooden boats that had been sold or were being taken away for repairs. He has moved *Kitty Hawk*, which once belonged to Orville Wright, and he once moved a Chinese junk; his father, who founded the trucking firm, once moved a 56-foot steamship from Lake Muskoka to Lake of Bays, mounting it on a giant sled and towing it across snow-covered roads.

"What I knew about wooden boats," Paul said, "is that you couldn't sleep the night before a move for fear you'd scratch them."

Then, in 1994, Hammond got a call from Ruby Budd. Her husband, Aud, had recently passed away, and Ruby wondered if Paul would like to buy Aud's old boat. Paul had heard of the boat from Ruby and Aud's daughter, who had worked for him for many years.

He was intrigued, and agreed to visit Ruby at her home in Milford Bay, a few minutes from Bracebridge on Lake Muskoka.

The boat was stored in a single slip boathouse which had been built to house the 28-foot boat and not much else. A single light bulb hanging from a cord was the only illumination, but it was enough to reveal a large boat hanging in a sling above the water. The leather upholstery was cracked, the canvas "navy top" was decayed, and there looked to be at least an inch of dust on the boat. The motor was completely seized, and the hull was so dry "you could have thrown a cat through the cracks," Paul said, but it seemed to be in restorable shape so he agreed to buy it.

The lettering on the hull revealed that the boat was named *Onweglyde III*, but what kind of boat was it? There was no maker's plate on the dash, no initials or signature written anywhere that could be seen. So who had built this boat, and when? Ruby had no idea — the boat had been her father-in-law's, and had been in the boathouse when she and Aud had married nearly 50 years earlier. Although she lived beside the water, she had no love of it and certainly had no interest in boats. So in between tinkering with the motor, and waiting for the hull planks to soak up enough water to swell the cracks closed, Paul began to ask around.

Some said the boat was a Ditchburn, looking at the lines of the deck and the shape of the windshield. But that didn't seem right. The lines were similar, but the finishing touches weren't as fine as a Ditchburn. Others, old-timers who lived in the Milford Bay area, said the boat was built by Aud and his father, Herb Budd. That seemed to

Another fine example of a boat painted in its environment, Onweglyde III looks absolutely at home in a shallow bay, the water translucent and limpid, the boat seeming to hover above the bottom rather than merely float.

make sense. Both Aud and Herb had been house and cottage painters, but they were also renowned as boat finishers. They stripped and revarnished boats that were showing the effects of the sun, and in the earlier years they had done custom finishing work for some of the smaller boat building shops in the area, the places that produced a couple of boats a season and didn't require the services of a full-time varnisher. They would have needed a boat to get to painting jobs — in fact, it wasn't unusual to see four or five ladders lashed to the rails of the boat's navy top, and there was still a paint-stained sheet of linoleum on the floor where the paint cans were piled. So wouldn't they have spent a quiet winter building their own boat?

Hammond began to share that theory around, to see whether others thought it made sense. Aud's brother-in-law, Lionel Cope, certainly did not agree. "He laughed," Paul said. "He said 'They couldn't build a boat! They couldn't drive a nail straight. They were painters.'" Lionel had worked as a boat-varnisher in Port Carling for many years, and seemed a reliable source. He told Paul the boat wasn't a Budd boat, it was a Clive Brown, and Herb Budd had acquired it from Brown as part of some sort of deal in the 1920s.

In the first half of the 20th century, there were dozens of small boat builders plying their trade in Muskoka. Most have been forgotten, some with good reason, but a few like Clive Brown stood out. In the workshop behind his home on McMurray Street in Bracebridge, he produced a couple of dozen gorgeous launches for wealthy clients. Fiercely independent, refusing even to have an assistant and certainly not willing to have an employer, Brown was nonetheless revered as a master builder and a perfectionist. Some of his clients were wealthy and powerful seasonal residents who knew their boats and valued craftsmanship — Brown built for renowned families such as the Mellons of Pittsburgh, and for people like Carl Borntraeger and Nelson Davis, whose knowledge of wooden boats made their collections famous in boating circles. He also built more modest vessels, cedar and mahogany runabouts that were every bit as well built but whose finishing touches were a bit more modest than the millionaires' boats.

Whatever he built, though, Brown poured into it both his craftsmanship and his eccentricities. His designs may not have varied much from those being used by the larger builders, but his techniques make his boats unmistakable to those who study the details. Hammond enlisted the help of some of those detail-oriented people, and a consensus began to emerge. Boat restoration experts studied the construction of Paul's boat, looking at the pattern of the frames and the way planks were attached with the same degree of care an archaeologist would use to decide whether an arrowhead was carved by a Mohawk or an Ojibwa hunter. Where others could see the fine lines and delicate shape that marks a boat as being Muskoka-built, they noted the use of bolts rather than clench nails to fasten the planks, and other details that made the boat unique. And they concluded that *Onweglyde III* is almost certainly a Clive Brown, likely built in the late-teens or early-twenties.

There are still mysteries attached to the boat: who was the boat built for, and what happened to *Onweglyde I* and *II*? How did the Budds come to have as their workboat a fine launch that, even at the prices Brown charged, could have been beyond their means and certainly was beyond their needs? It seems unlikely those questions will ever be answered. When Brown died in 1959, the Budds had already been using the *Onweglyde* for nearly 30 years; anyone who knew the details of its origins has long since disappeared.

In the 1990s, Paul Hammond registered the *Onweglyde III* for the Antique and Classic Boat Society's annual show. When he arrived, he was presented with a paper sheet to place on the seat: *Onweglyde III*, it read, built circa 1920 by Clive Brown. Sometimes, it seems, nearly certain is as close as one is going to get.

This is a painting of the owners as much as it is a painting of the boat. Ted and Loretta Rogers have owned Brown Bear *since it was new.*
Loretta Rogers uses the boat regularly, but it's a rare occasion when Ted Rogers takes the wheel. On this day, Dunford said,
Ted Rogers embraced the drive with passion, and kept smiling about it for hours afterward.

19   The Last of Its Breed

On a hot July afternoon, a wooden boat roars toward the north end of Lake Rosseau. It's fast and moves cleanly, cutting easily through the chop at 30 miles an hour. The lines of the boat are unusual and challenge observers who try to identify it. The bow is sharp and narrow, with a long nose that extends several feet over the water, but just aft of the bow the hull quickly bellies out in a graceful compound curve. There are angular lines that were not seen in the 1930s and 40s, but the boat still has a softer, more curvaceous look than is typical of the late era wooden boats. It is a Greavette Executive, one of only five believed to have been built, and it is the last model that bore the renowned Greavette name.

By 1973, when this boat was built, there was little that remained of the once-proud Muskoka boat-building industry. Ditchburn and Minett-Shields were merely distant memories, and most of the smaller boat shops that still existed had turned their attention to restoration work. But Greavette still soldiered on, building and selling new wooden boats. Tom Greavette himself passed away in 1958, and the company had been sold to brothers Herman and Jack Heintzman of Toronto. They were renowned piano builders whose great-grandfather had founded the company they in turn ran, but Herman in particular loved boats as much as pianos. He built a couple of boats himself, and befriended famed racer Harold Wilson who had won world championships in Greavette boats in the 1930s. When the Greavette company came up for sale, Herman could not resist. For more than ten years he ran both the piano firm and the boatworks, often leaving his Toronto office on a Thursday afternoon

and flying his own plane from Toronto Island Airport to Muskoka, where he would spend three days in the boatworks. He was ably assisted by general manager Ron McNab, who had worked for Tom Greavette and who was married to Greavette's daughter, Lorraine.

When Herman died in 1969, his widow Ann decided to sell the boatworks and focus on the piano business instead. Bruce Wilson, a Toronto businessman who wanted to move to Muskoka, purchased Greavette as a means of making that move feasible. The company was rich in history and retained a skilled workforce of a dozen or so people, but the competition with fibreglass boats was battering its sales. Wilson knew that there were only two ways to make money in the boat business — build lots of inexpensive boats, or build a few high-end boats. The fibreglass companies had the inexpensive lines tied up, but he had high hopes for the Greavette Executive. It was designed to be a floating living room, equipped with soft, comfortable seats and luxurious features that would evoke memories of Greavette's glory years. For at least one customer, the combination was irresistible.

Ted Rogers was not yet a household name in Canada — his eponymous cable network was still a year away, and the mobile phones he would champion were found only in the imagination of science fiction writers — but the 40-year-old businessman was already successful enough to be part of Greavette's target market. He had the two things boat builders have always liked in their clients: a desire to own a wooden boat, and the means to own a good one. Rogers had been eyeing wooden boats for years, telling himself he would buy one when he got a chance. In 1973, he decided the time was right, and he purchased a brand new Greavette Executive.

He chose well, for the Greavette Executive was a good boat. Solidly built of mahogany, it had a feel and class that far outstripped the plywood and wood/fibreglass hybrids that were also being produced at that time. The hull was well designed, slicing neatly through the water and offering a smooth yet fun ride, and the V-8 Crusader inboard/outboard was fast and reliable.

It should have been a popular boat, and those who bought it, liked it. But there were too few buyers. It was the lowest time in wooden boat circles, when new boats were largely unsellable and old boats were not yet collectible.

In the U.S., a handful of boating fans had begun to rediscover the allure of the old wooden boats. They'd even started getting together with other boat-lovers to admire the launches their parents and grandparents had owned. Many Canadian boaters were amused by this trend — they had wooden boats too, but the boats were still being used, treated as functional vessels rather than as collectible items. The first wooden boat shows would not take place in this country for another decade. Even if the antique wooden boats had been popular in the early 1970s, it's still doubtful whether the Greavette Executive would have sold widely. Anyone with the money to buy new was simply more likely to buy a new fibreglass boat. "It

was just the end of an era," Bruce Wilson would say some years later. "Glass boats were taking over, and that was it."

Only five Greavette Executives were sold. And in 1974, the year after Ted Rogers bought his brand new Greavette, the company stopped making new boats and focused entirely on restoration work. By the end of the decade, it closed its doors for good.

The Rogers family continued to enjoy their new boat, joking that they were among the few people to have bought an antique boat when it was brand new. The children named it *Brown Bear*, and it was used to visit neighbours, to go for cruises, and to skip handily across the lake. "It's easy to handle, and it rides well," said Loretta Rogers. As for speed, it certainly holds its own against newer fibreglass boats. "This one keeps up with them," she said. "You don't realize how fast you're going because it's such a smooth ride. You're not feeling the bump-bump-bump with each extra mile an hour."

There are some investments that make sense right away, and others that take time. Buying a new wooden boat in 1973 was seen as a quirky way to spend money, but time has proven Ted and Loretta Rogers right. Most of the fibreglass boats built that year have long since been abandoned, their gel coat surfaces pitted and crazed, their fibreglass hulls blistered by pox and saturated with core rot. But *Brown Bear* is still treasured, and she has surely earned the right to be called a classic.

20 The Unforgettable First Love

There is no love like your first love, no romance quite as sweet and enduring as a romance that begins in youth. Whether the object of your affection is a person or a boat, the fact remains the same: even after a lifetime of other loves, the sight of your first love can still catch your breath.

John Callaghan wasn't even born when *Neriva* was built, but he came to love the boat as he grew up. She was his grandfather's boat, and some of his earliest memories are of sitting on his grandfather's lap, peering between the spokes in the steering wheel as *Neriva* carried the family on a quiet cruise around Bala Bay. Callaghan's grandfather bought *Neriva* in 1924 for the sum of $900. The boat was advertised as used, but nobody's quite sure who used it, or exactly when it was built. The builders are known, though — Oliver McNeil and Bill Norris, brothers-in-law who ran a marina, garage and taxi stand in Bala in the 1920s and '30s. Boat building was Bill Norris's sideline, something he did in the winter to keep himself busy and bring in a bit of money. Norris and a helper turned out one launch a year, while McNeil spent his winters prospecting, but the boats — like the marina and the garage — bore the names of both McNeil and Norris.

Like many small builders, McNeil and Norris purchased hull designs, then built using their instincts and their knowledge of what had worked for other builders. The result was boats that can be hard to identify. To some eyes the *Neriva* looks a bit like a Ditchburn. Others say it's more like Minett's work. The hardware doesn't help in identifying the boat, either. McNeil and Norris didn't have the means to have elements like cleats and window brackets custom made; they simply bought what they could get from marine suppliers. The *Neriva* has Ditchburn cleats, and an attractive bow light with a unique, flat top that is sometimes seen on Minett boats. But Bert Minett usually encased the light in a carved, teardrop moulding, giving it a luxurious and finished touch. Bill Norris wasn't building luxury boats, he was building for the mid-range buyer who just wanted a boat that performed well and looked good. His bow light is simply fastened to the deck without the wood trim.

The *Neriva* was an attractive boat, though, pretty and well composed with a pronounced tumblehome at the stern that gives it a distinctive set of "hips." It rides well, and the cut of the bow throws a distinctive cowlick of water that is a pleasure to watch. Callaghan recalls one evening in his teens when he was waved over by a man sitting on his dock. "I see this boat go by all the time," the man said, "and it's just the prettiest riding boat I've ever seen."

But looks and a pleasant ride weren't enough to keep the *Neriva* in prized condition, and by 1965 the boat was derelict. It changed hands at least three times over the next 20 years before it was finally restored in the late 1980s. Its original beauty intact again, and renamed *Ariel* for the water sprite in Shakespeare's *The Tempest*, it caught the eye of Joe and Sally Gladden. Residents of Atlanta, Georgia, the Gladdens had been touring Muskoka hoping to find a Greavette Streamliner. When they saw the McNeil and Norris boat, they

Dunford usually works on canvas, but occasionally will paint on masonite. The smooth surface of the masonite allows him to add even more detail than can be included on a textured surface like canvas. This painting of Neriva is an extreme example. Much of it was painted under a jeweller's magnifier. The boat on the other side of the dock is Clarie II, a 1920 Great Lakes Gold Cup racer that is regularly seen cruising the Muskoka lakes.

changed their plans. "We opened up the boathouse and there she was," said Joe Gladden. "There was a beam of sunlight streaming in, and my wife said 'this is it.'" The *Ariel* was soon plying the waters of a small mountain lake in Georgia where the Gladdens have a cottage.

Callaghan, meanwhile, had reached the age when a man begins to reconsider the lost loves of his youth, and he wondered what had ever become of his grandfather's boat. It wasn't a burning passion, just a persistent curiosity, but one night he read in a boat directory that someone in Georgia owned a McNeil and Norris. There are only three McNeil and Norris boats known to exist, so Callaghan called the Gladdens.

Not only was it the same boat, but Joe Gladden said they had just brought the boat back to Muskoka, to use it at their Lake Rosseau cottage. And so, on a summer's evening three-quarters of a century after his grandfather had bought it, Callaghan once again sat behind the wheel of *Neriva*. As he pulled away from the dock, the half-remembered smells and sights brought the memories flooding back. Even the handling remained the same, the boat giving a familiar shudder that indicated the grease cup in the stuffing box was running low.

"This was the boat I drove when I was 14, my grandfather's boat," said Callaghan. "There's a picture of 14 grandchildren piled in and on this boat. When I saw it, there was a tear in my eye."

The Gladdens eventually decided to sell the boat — like many people who love old boats, they had become "overboated," Joe said, and had run out of slip space. It was obvious who would buy it, and a deal was quickly reached with Callaghan. "I couldn't imagine it being anywhere else," said Gladden.

The wicker chairs confirmed that decision. For as long as they had owned the boat, the Gladdens had been looking for a pair of wicker chairs like the ones that must have been in the boat when it was new. They had to be narrow to fit the narrow boat, and their like couldn't be found anywhere. Without them, the vessel just wasn't complete. But not long after he bought the boat, Callaghan invited Gladden to come and see the chairs. They had been removed from the boat in his grandfather's day, and placed in the cottage next door. Callaghan had simply knocked on his next door neighbour's door and asked if he could buy them back.

The chairs were carried over to the boathouse, and nestled in place. The *Neriva* had truly come home.

21

Respectable at Last

"They sure look pretty when they're in the water, all dressed up."

I n the community of wooden boat-lovers, there will always be those who dislike certain boats. The lines that one person admires as muscular and brawny are dismissed by another as being coarse; the exuberant use of chrome hardware on one boat is pooh-poohed by a boat-lover who admires a more Spartan style of ornamentation.

In some circles, cedar strip boats have not earned even that sort of respect. On a lake crowded with Ditchburns and Minetts, a simple cedar strip fishing boat was once too utilitarian to be held in contempt, too plain to be noticed, too ordinary to warrant enmity. Like the aluminum and fibreglass fishing boats that they preceded, the cedar strip runabouts were regarded as functional boats at the purest level, designed and built for the simple purpose of carrying anglers on the water, or hauling gear to and from an island cottage. In the spring they were dragged into the water and submerged — often filled with stones to keep them underwater until the boards soaked up enough water to swell tight. In the fall they were hauled out again, flopped over onto a pair of sawhorses, and covered with a tarp for the winter. Some might be built better than others, but a well-built fishing boat was simply one that didn't leak. Or so it seemed.

But somewhere along the way, a funny thing happened to these supposedly utilitarian boats: they became beautiful.

Cedar strip boats have been around since the First World War, when outboard motors became small enough and reliable enough to be used by anyone other than a mechanical tinkerer. The vessel is held together in the same fashion as a canoe, planks fastened to numerous thin ribs rather than heavy frames. The entire structure of the boat is visible at a glance. The expensive mahogany launches were built with cockpits for drivers and passengers, and a separate compartment for the inboard engine, a design that allows — even demands — fine cabinetry and upholstery that conveys a feeling of comfort, if not downright luxury. Outboard runabouts, on the other hand, were designed to maximize the usable space on board and minimize the time required to build them. There is no need for upholstery or fancy cabinetwork

That was just fine for some boat builders, whose main focus was assembling a usable, inexpensive boat that could be sold cheaply and used roughly. But there were always other builders, people who could see the potential for beauty in any boat — mahogany launch, canvas canoe, or cedar strip outboard runabout — and who were willing to put in extra effort and care to bring that beauty into existence. As with so much that begins its existence as a simple utilitarian object, in the hands of a dedicated craftsman the cedar strip boat began to acquire a certain dignity. Builders like Peterborough and Lakefield brought style and artistry to some of their designs, and built their boats with finesse and skill. Their more luxurious models didn't just have decks, steering wheels, windshields and cockpits, they had elegant lines with compound curves and they gleamed beneath multiple coats of varnish.

They were still relatively inexpensive compared to the mahogany launches and gentleman's racers, but they had a style and grace all their own. What's more, they survived and thrived even as the more expensive boats went into decline. The sweeping changes of the 20th century gradually brought an end to the construction of high-end wooden launches. The Depression drove some boat builders into bankruptcy. Then came the Second World War, with its attendant shortages in engines, fuel, and skilled workers. And after the war, just as prosperity was returning to the boat building industry, new materials entered the fray. Aluminum fabricators, faced with excess capacity now that their materials were no longer needed for armaments, discovered that their metal made excellent boat hulls. Fibreglass, invented in 1938 as an insulation material, was soon being used to build boats that made traditional wooden launches look old-fashioned and rather quaint. One by one, the old builders stopped production or adopted the new methods, and until the restoration boom hit in the 1980s, hardly anyone was building traditional wooden launches.

But through it all, there was still a home for cedar strip boats. For part of the 1950s, in fact, the Peterborough Canoe Company was the largest boat builder in the country, and every lake in Muskoka seemed to be home to a few cedar strip boats. The market for them certainly declined as more and more people began buying aluminum or fibreglass boats, but others recognized that a wooden boat still served its purpose perfectly well. The material was durable and easy to repair when damaged. Some fishing lodges found that their fleet of wooden rental boats actually lasted longer than similar boats made of aluminum and fibreglass. Because they were fairly quick to build and didn't require exotic materials, cedar strip boats even remained competitively affordable.

Most of the cedar strip builders eventually closed down, but a few — a very few, admittedly — remained in business. And even when wooden boats were at their nadir, one could still buy a brand new cedar strip boat from a firm like Giesler, which is still building boats at its plant north of Muskoka just as it has for more than 80 years.

It's said that a rising sea lifts all ships, and that's certainly true of the rising interest in wooden boats. Greavettes and Minetts are popular again, but so too are cedar strip boats. The high end models are being restored and copied, collected and displayed at shows. Even the utilitarian fishing boats have acquired an air of respectability they didn't have in the early days.

Like much in the world of wooden boats, there is nostalgia at play here as boat owners find themselves yearning to own once again a boat like the one they grew up with. Economics also enters into it — you can no longer pick up an abandoned Ditchburn for a few thousand dollars, but old cedar strip boats can still be hauled out of the woods for free. Even brand new cedar strip boats range from inexpensive — the highest-priced model Giesler sells is $3,600 — to moderately priced. And on a lake dominated by aluminum and fibreglass there is a recognition of the inherent beauty in a wooden boat — any wooden boat, no matter how humble. The variable texture of the material, the way it glows in the right light, the life itself that exists in wood grants dignity to the boats and makes them worthy of attention.

Doug Dunford has spent years painting the wooden boats of Muskoka, studying them from every conceivable angle. He has certainly earned the right to be blasé about some boats, dismissive of any that don't measure up. Yet he too can be captivated by the sight of a simple cedar strip boat like the one he painted from a scene on Lake Rosseau. "I'll never forget that scene. I drove by and there was an old fishing boat with a couple of people fishing," he said. "The sun had gone down pretty well and there was a kind of twilight — not really dark out yet but there were those rich blues you get in the sky at that time."

The boat was a Giesler — the same as his own — but what captivated him was not the familiarity of the boat but of the scene. It was, he said, something he himself had lived, and something which has been taking place in central Ontario's lake lands for many decades. "That was the boat that you saw growing up in cottage country, spending all your summers there. And I had this feeling of a father giving his son his first boat, an old wooden fishing boat."

Like many children of cottage country, Dunford finds his appreciation for the old fishing boats is growing as the years pass. "I just think they're such a pretty boat. I know they're not fancy like a Ditchburn or a Minett-Shields, but they still have their own character."

"It's neat now how people are starting to fix them up. It must be a hell of a lot of work, and you really don't get a whole lot at the end because it's still just an old fishing boat. There's not a great value put on them, but they sure look pretty when they're in the water, all dressed up."

Bibliography

The following books proved useful in researching this book, and we offer our thanks to the authors.

Beaumaris. By Patricia Ahlbrandt (Boston Mills Press, 1989)

Boats Unlimited. By Harold Wilson (Boston Mills Press, 1990)

Celebrating 25 Years. By members of the Antique and Classic Boat Society Toronto (2005)

Classic American Runabouts: Wood Boats, 1915-1965. By Phillip Ballantyne (MBI Publishing, 2004)

Ditchburn Boats: A Muskoka Legacy. By Harold Shield and Bev McMullen (Boston Mills Press, 2002)

Hackercraft. By James P. Barry (MBI Publishing, 2002)

Port Carling: Hub of the Lakes. By Richard Tatley (Stoddart, 1996)

The Boatbuilders of Muskoka. By A.H. Duke and W.M. Gray (Boston Mills Press, 1985)

The Canoe: A Living Tradition. By John Jennings (Firefly Books, 2002)

The Steamboat Era in The Muskokas. By Richard Tatley (Stoddart, 1983)

The Wooden Boat. By Joseph Gribbins (Friedman/Fairfax, 2001)

Wood and Glory. By William Gray and Timothy Du Vernet (Boston Mills Press, 1997)

In addition, reference was made to various issues of the following periodicals:

Bracebridge Examiner
Bracebridge Herald-Gazette
Classicboat
Muskoka Lakes Association Yearbook
Muskoka Life
The Muskokan
The Muskoka Sun
Toronto Telegram
Wooden Boat
Yachting

Index of Boats

Acknowledgements

Completing a book requires the support of a tremendous number of people, and *Grace & Speed* is no exception. Thanks are due first of all to Murray Walker, who had the vision for this project, who guided it through to completion, and who was always willing to share his vast knowledge and boundless enthusiasm for the boats of Muskoka.

Designer Gill Stead and editor Lynn Roberts both performed sterling work. Without their skills, a manuscript could not have been turned into the book you hold in your hands. Photographer Kelly Holinshead brought her talents to bear, capturing the images of Doug Dunford at work and photographing his paintings. Thanks also to photographer Karen Genovese, who allowed Doug to work from her photograph of *Miss Canada III*.

None of this would have been possible without the assistance of the people who own these boats, and those who have studied them. They let us see, photograph and ride in their boats, and they freely shared the stories they had accumulated over the years. More importantly, the owners of these boats recognize that they are not just property owners; they are custodians of our shared boating heritage. Many have contributed heavily to ensure that these boats survive. For preserving and protecting these vessels, these works of art, we all owe them our thanks.

Among those who shared their knowledge, their time, or their boats are:

Bill and Eileen Bartells
Sally Boothby
Mike Borneman
Bob Breadner
Peter Breen
John Callaghan
Tim Chisholm
George Cuthbertson
Gary DeGroote

Graeme and Phyllis Ferguson
John Finlay
Karen and Bobby Genovese
Rolf Gerling
Ted and Sharon Johnson
Joe and Sally Gladden
Jerry Hamlin
Paul Hammond

Murray Hogarth
Brian and Sharon McGrath
Rick McGraw
Katherine Gerling-McLeod
Stan Meek
Hugh and Eliza Nevin
James Potter
Robert Purves
Ted and Loretta Rogers

Lloyd and Susan Ross
George Rossiter
Will Ruch
Peter and Lydia Sharpe
Eva Shields
Ed Skinner
Cliff Stanton
Joe Walton
Roger Werner

There is no better place in Muskoka to celebrate the region's famed waterway heritage than on the shores of Muskoka Bay. For generations, visitors arrived in Muskoka aboard trains that pulled out onto the Muskoka Wharf, where they could board the steamships that would take them to their hotels. The site was home to two of the greatest boatworks — Ditchburn and Greavette — and many of their famed boats were tested in the waters of Muskoka Bay.

The boatworks are gone, and so too is the railway track, but the steamships remain, and the rich heritage continues to be celebrated at Grace & Speed: Muskoka Boat and Heritage Centre.

The 24,000 square foot centre traces Muskoka's history by looking at the steamships, the hotels, and the boat builders who made the region famous. The interactive exhibits, the boathouse housing an in-water display of gorgeous wooden boats, and the ever-expanding reference library make this site an essential place for any lover of wooden boats to visit.